Ad

As India gets globally inte grated, its and m is also
spreading all over the world ranging from yoga and meditation
to inner engineering. My congratulations to Professor Sheth and
Mr. Gyanendra Singh for documenting the role of leadership in
transforming India to become the third-largest economy in the world.

– Sadhguru, Founder, Isha Foundation

Prof Jagdish N. Sheth is a globally renowned management guru who
has influenced academic discourse around the world with his original
insights into consumer behaviour, business strategy and the impact
of geopolitical developments. I have had the privilege of benefitting
immensely from his wisdom. He has always remained an eternal
optimist about India's potential to emerge as a global economic
power.

In this compelling exposition of India's Road to Transformation, Prof
Sheth, along with his co-author Gyanendra Singh, has chronicled the
nation's remarkable rise from a fledgling state struggling to find its
feet to a flourishing economic powerhouse that is making its mark
on the global stage. He also identifies the factors that are critical to
sustaining this rise and ensuring its prosperity benefits every citizen. I
strongly recommend this book to Indian and foreign readers.

– Mukesh Ambani, Chairman & MD, Reliance Industries

India's Road to Transformation is a spellbinding story of India's
transformation from a low-tech to a high-tech nation and from a
domestically isolated to a globally integrated economy. India is
destined to become the third largest economy in the world as it
becomes a global sourcing destination for global enterprises. It is also
destined to become the service capital of the world. Professor Sheth
and Mr Singh are master storytellers!

– Anand Mahindra, Chairman, Mahindra Group

Congratulations to Jagdish Sheth and Gyanendra Singh for their moving story of India's recent transformation. In my previous talks in India, I would raise the question "When will the Indian Tiger wake up?" Surely, India's leaders must have been miffed seeing the rapid economic rise of its neighbors such as China, Vietnam, South Korea, Singapore, and Indonesia. Now India can add its name because its economic engine has turned on thanks to Prime Minister Narendra Modi. Much more has to be done! All the needed reforms and steps are made clear in this brilliant analysis of India's ongoing transformation.

**– Philip Kotler, Author, Marketing Professor,
Economist and Consultant**

In 2023, I had the privilege to meet Prime Minister Narendra Modi in Delhi. He is an extraordinary world leader and I am sure India will become a super economic power under his pragmatic leadership. My congratulations to Professor Sheth and Mr. Singh for documenting India's transformative journey.

– Congressman Richard McCormick

'India's Road to Transformation: Why Leadership Matters' provides insight into the long overdue attention to India's economy and the pivotal role Prime Minister Modi played in this growth. Backed by compelling facts, the book highlights key achievements, such as a stable interest rate regime, robust foreign exchange reserves, increased foreign direct investments, and a vibrant local startup ecosystem. The book serves as an insightful resource for anyone seeking to understand India's economic transformation and its potential as a global powerhouse and a key source for human talent.

**– Dipak C. Jain, Honorary Vice Chancellor, JIO University,
Past Dean at INSEAD and Kellogg School of Management**

Congratulations to Professors Sheth and Singh for documenting the extraordinary leadership of Prime Minister Modi in transforming India for the 21st century and to aspire the nation to become the third largest economy of the world. 'India's Road to Transformation' is a must read for students of management.

– Shashi Kiran Shetty, Chairman, Allcargo Group

'India's Road to Transformation: Why Leadership Matters' is an essential book to understand the key role played by resolute national leadership. It makes a compelling case that continuity matters, using comparative cases like South Korea, Singapore, among others. As such, it is a distinguished contribution to the political economy literature focused on India and based on the deep combined experience of its authors.

– John R. McIntyre, PhD, Professor of Management and International Affairs, Executive Director at Georgia Tech CIBER

This page is intentionally left blank

VIBRANT
PUBLISHERS

INDIA'S
ROAD TO
TRANSFORMATION:
WHY LEADERSHIP MATTERS

Documenting Prime Minister Narendra Modi's pragmatic
leadership to transform India into a superpower!

DR. JAGDISH N. SHETH
GYANENDRA SINGH

India's Road to Transformation: Why Leadership Matters

Paperback ISBN 10: 1–63651–227–5
Paperback ISBN 13: 978–1–63651–227–3

Ebook ISBN 10: 1–63651–229–1
Ebook ISBN 13: 978–1–63651–229–7

Hardback ISBN 10: 1–63651–228–3
Hardback ISBN 13: 978–1–63651–228–0

Vibrant Publishers books are available at special quantity discount for sales promotions, or for use in corporate training programs. For more information please write to bulkorders@vibrantpublishers.com

Please email feedback / corrections (technical, grammatical or spelling) to spellerrors@vibrantpublishers.com

To access the complete catalogue of Vibrant Publishers, visit
www.vibrantpublishers.com

*"This book is dedicated to my co-author,
Gyanendra (Gyani) Singh who passed away
before the book was published. Gyani was simply
brilliant and very passionate about India.
It was indeed my privilege to be his co-author."*

– Jagdish N. Sheth

This page is intentionally left blank

About the Authors

 **Prof. (Dr.) Jagdish N. Sheth** is Charles H. Kellstadt Professor of Business at the Goizueta Business School at Emory University. He is globally known for his scholarly contributions to consumer behavior, relationship marketing, competitive strategy, and geopolitical analysis. Professor Sheth has over 50 years of combined experience in teaching and research at the University of Southern California, the University of Illinois at Urbana-Champaign, Columbia University, MIT, and Emory University. Dr. Sheth has been on the board of several companies including Norstan, Pacwest-Telecom, Cryocell International, Shasun Drugs and Chemicals, and WIPRO Limited. Over the 50 years, he has been an advisor to numerous companies including Whirlpool, Motorola, Texas Instruments, Cox Communications, Rockwell International, AT&T, Bellsouth, WIPRO Consumer Care, Aditya Birla Group, L.M. Mittal (Avanta), E&Y, Square D, Ingan Micro, Hughes Corporation, and others.

He is the founder of In-Core, a consulting and advisory services company that has focused on telecommunications, cable, and IT services. His book *Rule of Three* has been the foundation for investment bankers, industry consolidation, and horizontal mergers and acquisitions.

Dr. Sheth has been an advisor to the Singapore Government in repositioning the nation for the future. He has also been the policy advisor to the US Government about the future of the telecommunications industry. He is the Founder of the Center for Telecommunications Management (CTM) at the University of Southern California (USC) which has now become an Institute. He is also the Founder and Chairman of the India, China, and America (ICA) Institute which analyzes the trilateral relationship and its impact globally on geopolitics, security, trade, and investment. Professor Sheth and his wife, Madhu Sheth, have established the Sheth Family Foundation to promote India and its culture in the United States. They have also established the Madhuri and Jagdish Sheth Foundation to support scholars and scholarship in the field of marketing. Finally, Professor Sheth is the Founder and Chairman of the Academy of Indian Marketing (AIM) which supports research and scholarship among Indian scholars in marketing and management.

 Former P&G executive, Managing Partner at The Partnering Group, and Director of the Center for Retail Management at the Kellogg School of Management, **Late Gyanendra Singh** (1945-2024) had a diverse career spanning the globe. He graduated from BITS (Pilani) in 1968 with a degree in Chemical Engineering and received his MS and MBA degrees from the University of Illinois in 1970 and 1971. He served in Product Development, Marketing, and Management Systems for P&G in the US and Japan during 1971-93 before entering the consulting and academic world. His initial career in R&D led to two patents and new products. This was followed by a marketing and management systems career, during which his

strategic insights led to many concepts of Category Management. As a pioneer of Category Management, he has authored many articles and books and advised multinationals across the globe – from Argentina to Russia during 1993-2010. Subsequently, his work has focused on change management within large organizations, including national transformation. He passed away in January 2024 before the book's release.

This page is intentionally left blank

Table of Contents

This page is intentionally left blank

Preface: Why this book?

From Dr. Jagdish N. Sheth

I left India in 1961 to pursue an MBA degree at the University of Pittsburgh and continued my doctoral education in behavioral sciences. I returned to India in 1968 as a visiting professor at IIM Calcutta under a grant from the Ford Foundation. When I left India, there was a chronic shortage of consumer durable products. For example, one had to wait for seven years for a scooter or a telephone.

Things had deteriorated especially in Bengal which was governed by the Communist Party and a strong Naxalite insurgence. The sidewalks were stacked up with garbage of four to seven feet. Many well-established companies were relocating from Calcutta to other cities including Bombay and New Delhi.

I came back in 1970 to teach a one-week executive development program on export marketing at the Administrative Staff College in Hyderabad. There was a strong anti-American sentiment in the country which led Coca-Cola, IBM, and General Motors to exit India. India's strategic partner was the Soviet Union and the Planning Commission was almighty. Basic infrastructure was stagnant and exports of Indian goods such as textiles and machine tools were unable to compete with Japan and eventually with China. There was a feeling of hopelessness and brain drain. This lasted for decades including a couple of wars with Pakistan and economic crises of Balance of Payments and lack of growth domestically.

The 1991 economic reforms resulted in the second independence. They unlocked India's economic potential.

Many industries were deregulated and allied with the private sector to compete with the monopoly of state enterprises, for example, the airline and the telecom industries.

At the same time, there was a mobile telephone revolution starting with feature phones and eventually expanding to smartphones. The wireless networks evolved from narrow to broadband and integrated with the world economy through e-commerce and social media.

The consumer demand shifted from unbranded to branded consumption and from unorganized retailing to organized retailing. India has now become the third-largest consumer market in the world based on purchasing power parity. There are growing choices of both domestic and international brands including in the third and fourth tier cities.

Most importantly, there is a growing positive self-image and "can do" attitude, especially after the success of entrepreneurs and digital platforms such as Aadhaar and UPI. There is excitement about the future potential of India and its leadership of the global south. The hosting of G20 in 2023 changed the image of the country from a country of roaming cows and snake charmers to a country of a talented pool of workers across professions and not limited to just IT services.

My visits to India became more frequent since I joined the board of directors as an independent board member of Wipro Limited in 1999. The impressive growth of IT services from Y2K outsourcing to a more than $150 billion industry in less than 30 years is simply amazing. India seems destined to become the service capital of the world and many multinationals will become the largest employers in accounting and software services.

As India repositions from a restricted domestic-centric economy to a globally integrated one and from a low-tech to a high-tech economy, it is likely to emerge as a new triad power consisting of China, the United States, and India. This new triad power will result in new geopolitical realignment and strategic partnership between the US and India to contain the military rise of China, especially in the Indo-Pacific region. The reduction of poverty and financial inclusion through Aadhaar and UPI public platforms will democratize the economy and generate more entrepreneurs across social strata.

Much of this can be attributed to political stability and continuity. But as described in our book, ultimately, it is the leadership that matters.

From Gyanendra Singh

I left India in 1968 after graduating from the Birla Institute of Technology & Science (BITS), Pilani to pursue graduate studies at the University of Illinois at Urbana-Champaign. During my time there, I worked for a very young Prof. Jagdish Sheth, already famous for his theory of consumer behavior, as his research assistant. Thus began a professional relationship that turned into a lifelong friendship. We stayed in touch even after I left Illinois to work for Procter & Gamble (P&G) both in the United States and Japan.

During my years with P&G, I did not have much time to visit India other than occasional trips that averaged once every three years. On each visit, I realized that India hardly seemed to change; its policymakers were content with their protectionist and socialist policies that emphasized self-sufficiency and distributing the national, economic pie without thinking much about enlarging it.

Leading economists accepted India's slow growth as inevitable – characterizing it as the "Hindu rate of growth"; as if Hinduism was incapable of moving fast or setting and achieving high goals, or its Hindu majority was holding it back. At the same time, one could see that Taiwan, South Korea, Hong Kong, and Singapore, nicknamed "Asian Tigers" were sprinting forward with very different policies – export-oriented capitalist policies that emphasized integration with world markets and encouraged foreign investments. Singapore and Hong Kong liberalized their trading regimes by establishing and actively promoting free trade. On the other hand, Taiwan and Hong Kong, owing to their small domestic markets, implemented export-centric policies intertwined with their foreign policies to create foreign, expanded markets for their locally made goods. For three decades, between the 1950s and 1990s, the four Asian Tigers were able to strategically grow their economies by 7.5% each year (CFI, 2020).

I gave up on my hopes of seeing rapid growth in India when it did not change its policies even after China seemingly learned from the "Asian Tigers" and transformed its policies under the leadership of Deng Xiaoping. Eventually, India's profligacy in fiscal management during the late 1980s led to the Balance of Payments (BoP) crisis of 1991, when the country didn't have sufficient foreign exchange reserves to make global payments for international trades, causing it to borrow $2.2 billion from IMF between 1991 and 1993 to open its economy to the world. This turned out to be a "blessing in disguise" since it shook India's policymakers, who had no choice but to accept reforms– because there was no other rational choice left.

In all fairness, the years of Fabian socialism under Congress rule were not without successes– the Indian economy did grow at 2–4% after Independence until 1980, and 4–6% during the 1980s, as compared to 1% under the British. In addition, the "Green Revolution" and "White Revolution" that brought self-sufficiency in agricultural and dairy products were major achievements. The problem was that, in comparison to India, other countries were growing much faster with different policies, while India was hobbled by its "License-permit Raj" across its industrial and service sectors. What ailed India's economy has been well documented in the book *India Unbound* by my good friend and former P&G-India CEO, Gurcharan Das.

I left P&G in 1993 to pursue my entrepreneurial interests. As part of this, I visited India in December 1994 to explore software development opportunities. I was pleasantly surprised by what I saw: India seemed to be changing. Entrepreneurship was visible, multinational companies that had earlier given up on India were back and, while there was considerable opposition to the new policies ushered in by the Congress government under the leadership of Prime Minister Narasimha Rao and Finance Minister Manmohan Singh, it seemed that India had indeed changed course.

This belief was reinforced during my next trip in December 1998 when the other national party of India–BJP under Atal Bihari Vajpayee–was in power. They had not only embraced the reforms but had accelerated the pace of reforms; infrastructure was being built, realignment of foreign policies was underway, and state socialism was being scaled back. India was set firmly on course during his term (1998–2004) even though an impatient electorate did not buy the premise of "India shining" campaign and returned power to the Congress-led coalition.

However, India continued onwards and upwards regardless of the change in government.

During the last two decades, I have visited India every year and with each visit lasting about three months, I have seen and experienced the transformative changes happening there. These "annual snapshots" of India's developmental journey have given me a good sense of India's unstoppable climb into the group of leading global powers. Prof. Sheth, of course, has continued to be involved with India throughout his academic career and consulting work, and his books such as *Chindia Rising* (among many others) have documented this journey.

India's journey has also been recognized internationally with India being grouped among the "BRIC" countries–Brazil, Russia, India, and China, as emerging powers since 2003. Subsequently, this group was formalized as BRICS, an international block with regular meetings, along with the addition of South Africa–the most dynamic economy in Africa. India also became a member of the G20 group of countries that replaced the earlier G7 after the Great Recession of 2008–09.

India's status as an emerging economic power seemed threatened during 2013–14 when India was being seen as among the "Fragile five" countries (Brazil, India, Indonesia, South Africa, and Turkey) at risk of imploding economically – with high deficits, inflation, policy paralysis, and corruption in high places. While India had progressed well during the first term of Manmohan Singh, it seemed to have regressed during its second term – again due to fiscal imprudence and distributive economic policies.

Fortunately, Indian electorates chose wisely, as they have done time and again despite the skeptics, and brought the BJP back to power under the new leadership of Narendra Modi. The new government has not only corrected the policy mistakes of the previous regime but relaunched stagnant schemes along with new initiatives and major reforms– such as GST (Goods & Services Tax), IBC (Insolvency & Bankruptcy Code), DBT (Direct Benefits Transfer). Foreign policy has also been reshaped. While India continues to pay lip service to its neutral stance, there is a clear recognition of where its international interests truly are, and India is a key member of the "quad" countries – the United States, Japan, Australia, and India – that is evolving into a strategic alliance to checkmate China's geopolitical aspirations in the Indo-pacific region. India is once again the focus of international agencies owing to its fast-growing economy and is likely to be among the top three by 2030. There is talk of the new Triad of China, United States, and India–with frequent reminders that it is only as it should be, as it was historically before the Industrial Revolution caused the West to surge ahead of China and India.

However, there is always the risk of predictions not coming true–for one reason or another– the most recent example being that of Japan. During the 1980s, many thought leaders saw the rise of Japan to become the number one in the world–books were written proclaiming the inevitability of Japan replacing the United States as the leading economic power. However, it did not happen: demographic stagnation, lack of innovation, rigid bureaucracy, and poor leadership are among the many factors that held Japan back. Similarly, while many see China eventually displacing the United States as the world's number one superpower, many believe that its political institutions and future demographics will prove to be insurmountable barriers.

Therefore, we raise key questions about the risks ahead in India's long journey to superpower status– which many believe is India's manifest destiny. Is India's rise inevitable, as some people suggest because India has progressed even under weak coalition governments? Or whether strong governments with committed leaders are necessary?

We believe that while India's progress is impressive, it is short of its potential. Its rise to global superpower status is not inevitable. To achieve transformation within a reasonable period, say 15 to 20 years further "deep and widespread reforms" are required–likely only possible under a transformational leader on the lines of Deng Xiaoping, Lee Kuan Yew, or Park Chung Hee. We delve into those questions by exploring why nation-building is so difficult and why it invariably requires transformational leadership, what are the lessons from history, and what are the characteristics of a transformational leader?

Specific to India, it is appropriate to ask how far India has come on its journey, how does Modi's term compares to previous regimes, what should India's transformation look like, and whether Modi is the "Transformational" leader that India needs at this point. If not Modi, then who else can rise to the challenge?

In drawing our conclusions, we have accessed four primary sources: two reports by PricewaterhouseCoopers (PwC), *re* *"World in 2050"* and *"India's winning leap"*– both available on the internet and from two recent books: *The Turn of the Tortoise* by T. N. Ninan and *India's Long Road: The Search for Prosperity*. For data, we have relied upon IMF and the World Bank, supplemented by rating agencies like Moody's or India's Niti Aayog– the Indian government's think tank. We have tried to summarize key points from our sources and for further details, we have referred our readers to these sources.

Introduction

In recent years, India has changed its foreign relations stance by becoming more vocal and actively participating in most global deliberations. Some experts believe that India is getting ready to assume the position of a key player in the world's politics and cross-continent sociopolitical discourse.

On June 2, 2023, Ajay Banga, an Indian, was selected as the 14th President of the World Bank Group. On December 1, 2022, for the first time ever, India assumed the presidency of G20, the bloc of 20, fast-growing economies in the world. Unlike before when India chose to sit on the fence when it came to international conflicts, India has publicly appealed to Israel to stop bombarding Gaza, and its support for the Palestinian Liberation Organization (PLO) remains unshaken.

However, successive Indian leaders or governments are fully aware that they need to build a strong, prosperous, and secure nation before India can successfully attain the enviable superpower status in the world.

In this book, we highlight the reasons why we strongly believe that India needs a transformative leader to maintain its current growth rate as well as develop its infrastructure rapidly in as few as 5-10 years from now to become a leading nation in the world.

By the end of this book, you will have learned some important leadership lessons about nation-building in the Indian context and what Indian people need to do right now to keep their country advancing, both economically and socio-politically.

In this book you will find cogent answers to the following questions:

- How was the Indian governance designed post-independence?

- Why has it been difficult to achieve a full-scale socioeconomic transformation in India?

- Who were the formidable Indian leaders who had contributed hugely to the country's current socioeconomic advancement?

- What kind of a leader does India need to sustain this high level of economic progress?

- How should the Indian people help their leaders stay the course and perpetuate a transformative leader who can get the job done?

Who can benefit from this book?

India's Road to Transformation: Why Leadership Matters, will be useful to:

- University professors who teach about Indian history, politics, economics, Indian foreign relations, and other aspects of India's advancement toward becoming an economic and political powerhouse.

- Students and researchers who are investigating or learning deeply about Indian nationhood.

- Indian local administrators or politicians who want to discover and implement some strategic steps needed by India to grow rapidly among the comity of nations.

- Foreign investors and entrepreneurs who want to be conversant with the recent developments in Indian business and other sectors before investing in the country.

- Any curious readers who aspire to know about India's current socioeconomic progress and the future steps it needs to take to become a superpower.

This page is intentionally left blank

Chapter 1

What Does Nation-Building Take – Why Is It More Complex than Business-Building?

World histories can testify to the fact that nation-building is a long, tedious journey – so long that many falter on their way to inspiring national transformation; even after a promising start, most countries and their ambitious leaders do not make it. Why is it mostly so?

The answer is threefold: it takes a long time, continuity matters, and you need a resolute transformational leader who is mission-driven. In this chapter, we will elaborate on why it takes time, why continuity matters, and why only "Transformational" leaders can achieve it.

Nation-building requires sustained efforts on multiple fronts – dealing with the internal and external environments or forces. The infrastructure has to be built, the institutions developed, the population upgraded, the economy improved, and all these essential steps would have to be carried out within the resource constraints and national priorities. In addition to these, efforts must be deployed towards taking care of national security and threats from foreign powers, as well as ensuring that competitive balance with other nations is at least maintained if not enhanced.

That these efforts have to be sustained while satisfying many different constituencies and stakeholders makes the task of nation-building enormously complex. Unlike a company, where the CEO has to deal primarily with his/her investors and shareholders, all of whom are committed to following the same financial goals of income and balance sheet, competition, and markets while meeting the company's obligations to society and environment, a nation has many more diverse stakeholders – different socioeconomic groups, demographics, ethnic and faith-based differences, public opinions and the media, not to mention a formidable opposition that wants to change the ruling dispensation at all times. The challenges are multiplied exponentially, analogous to solving a multi-dimensional problem instead of a single-dimensional one.

Continuity of leadership becomes critical in such dire situations; it takes time to develop a vision, convince followers that it is a vision worth embracing before they can put their unwavering support behind it, and show them how it can be achieved, all the while dealing with the opposition and the diverse stakeholders. While autocracies have the apparent advantage of being able to suppress dissidents or oppositions, and therefore achieving faster execution, democracies inevitably take longer in nation-building, although the foundations for progress are generally more solid having been built through compromises and consensus. However, this is not always the case: the level of success achieved during nation-building depends largely on the ability and skills of the leader. Therefore, managing change, especially during the critical transition period on the path to transformation, is an important prerequisite for successful nation-building.

Take two recent examples where continuity was critical, as was the ability to manage change: Mrs. Thatcher was able to do so in the United Kingdom in a democratic setup, even though Gorbachev could not in the Soviet Union despite its autocratic, single-party communist system. When Mrs. Thatcher came to power in 1979, after several years of lackluster conservative and labor leaders' performances (after Winston Churchill's second term ended in April 1955) and continuing policies of state domination of the economy that were implemented during the Attlee years immediately after the World War II, she faced enormous challenges to her authority. However, she was able to overcome the resistance to change through her resolute determination during the Falkland War which won her the public's admiration. More so, the positive economic outcomes arising from her policies of privatization and reduced state control revived hope in the British people. Her continuity during the long transition period was critical – she stayed at the helm for 11 years (1978-90).

On the other hand, Gorbachev was unable to continue for more than six years (1985-91) even though he had inherited an autocratic regime and a powerful vision. He chose political transformation over the economy and lost power before his policies *glasnost* and *perestroika* (Russian words for 'governmental openness and economic restructuring') could bear any fruit. In 1990, Gorbachev and Boris Yeltsin had jointly commissioned a group of economists to come up with an economic blueprint that would open the USSR to a European-like market economy, tagged *"500 Days Programme"*, but due to political pressure, Gorbachev did not support the economic experimentation, leaving the USSR's economy weakened and dilapidated. In any case, the transformation of the Soviet Union could not take place as the leaders of the 15 republics comprising the USSR bloc had lost interest in their Soviet supranational identity as they earnestly sought national economic solutions to the famine and death that was ravaging their people, eventually forcing Gorbachev-inspired policies to reverse course under the new leader – Boris Yeltsin.

Arguably, it may always be better to start with economic and social reforms before political reforms as Deng Xiaoping had demonstrated in China – because of the need to stay in power to provide the continuity needed for any transformation to occur. Deng, through his four-pronged socioeconomic agendas, otherwise known as the Four Modernizations, was able to ameliorate the problems caused by the excesses of Zedong Mao's Cultural Revolution. Deng Xiaoping engineered rapid economic developments in China by connecting his country to the rest of the world, creating avenues for sociocultural freedoms, and a better standard of living for the Chinese people.

Even when visionary leaders come to power, the challenges of building infrastructure within the fiscal and monetary constraints make it impossible to transform a nation in a short time. For the economy to grow at double-digit rates is seldom possible; even most high-growth economies achieve a 6–8% growth rate – doubling every 10 years at an average of 7%. The resources required to build an economy are always scarce and a perennial hurdle; the primary investment needed to jump-start an economy can only come from domestic savings plus foreign direct investments.

Research has shown that there is a direct relationship between savings and investments. Both private (household) and national savings could be indications of a rising economic growth pattern premised on the assumption that the disposal income rate has increased due to higher productivity growth and improved institutional functionality. As such, the investment rate will consequently spike in tandem, giving regions or nations with high savings rates the opportunity to grow very fast, as indicated in Figures 1.1 and 1.2 below.

Figure 1.1   **Gross Domestic Savings (% GDP)**

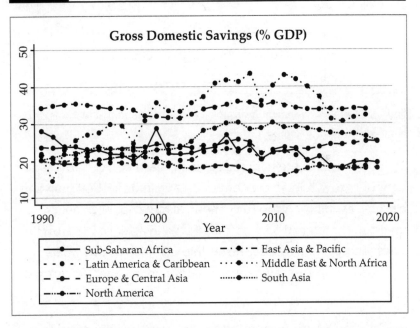

Source: World Development Indicators (WDI) data, modified by Kunal Sen and Abrams M.E. Tagem.

Figure 1.2   Gross Domestic Savings (% GDP) in SSA countries

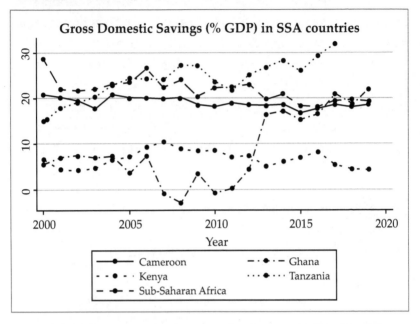

Source: World Development Indicators (WDI) data, modified by Kunal Sen and Abrams M.E. Tagem.

How much of the national savings could be injected to spur tangible growth in an economy? This is an important question because even high-growth economies have not been able to invest more than 30-35% of their GDPs to achieve 7% growth rates (except for a few countries like China that, during its hypergrowth years, averaged 40-50% savings and 10% growth rates).

On a more serious note, efforts to overcome the physical constraints seldom work. Even with the latest technologies, it takes time to build railroads, roadways, ports, waterways, airports, electricity grids, digital networks, etc. that a nation requires to grow, and for industries and its populace to take advantage of the new infrastructure. In circumstances where such efforts inevitably ignore fiscal and monetary limitations, it could lead to high inflation, currency devaluation, socioeconomic distress among the population, and regime change in democracies. Said simply, Rome was not built in a day!

It is also important to pay attention to the fact that demographic and social changes could impose additional constraints while making conscious attempts to build a nation. Even with significant investments in healthcare and education, it takes time before the next generation is healthier and better educated. For example, it takes 10 years to build institutions like the IITs, AIIMSs, or IIITs (Indian Institutes of Technology, All India Institutes of Medical Sciences, and Indian Institutes of Information Technology) – and such is the case in any country. In other words, there is always a gestation period for any new institutions to flourish.

Investments across different sectors also need to be prioritized and balanced; many communist/socialist countries have achieved high healthcare and education at the cost of high growth in their economies but the saddest aspect of this approach is that they have no jobs for their healthier populations – Cuba being the classic example. On the other hand, many countries, such as China and India, have attained high economic growth at the expense of their human development which has lagged these past years.

Changing social behavior is even more problematic; not only does it take time but it also creates fierce resistance to the ruling dispensation – especially in a democracy. The failure of population control in India and, in contrast, the persistence of the one-child norm in China, even after the abolition of the policy, are examples of the difficulty of changing human behavior. Even in autocratic societies, it can take a generation or more to achieve lasting social change. Any change in leadership or continuity of policies can reverse hard-won changes in social behavior. Hence, managing the balance between economic growth and social changes is critical, although the balancing, if shoddily implemented, may act as a brake on the nation-building processes.

To summarize: time, continuity, and transformational leadership are always needed for nation-building. More so, a clear vision, a feasible path to achieving that vision, and ensuring successful execution are the only ways through which this enormous task can be accomplished. Changes in the visions, policies, or programs can be very disruptive and can reverse progress. Even when the governing dispensation is the same, leadership changes generally lead to changes in directions; and the best possible scenario is for the same leader to take the nation to the next level – at least during such time when the original vision could be achieved.

If we accept the proposition that nation-building takes a long time and needs continuity and transformational leadership, the obvious question is: how much time is needed in general, and will be needed specifically for India to ascend to its next phase of significant transformation or growth?

The lessons of history suggest that the minimum time required for nation-building is around 15 years – this was the time required by Deng Xiaoping in China, Mustafa Kemal Ataturk in Turkey, and Helmut Kohl in Germany during the last century. Going back further in time, whether it was Napoleon, Genghis Khan, Caesar, or Alexander – all needed 15 years or more. Obviously, it can take less or more depending on the complexity of the situation, society, or the nation. There are notable exceptions, on the shorter side, four and five years respectively for Abraham Lincoln who saved the United States from disintegration during the Civil War while laying the foundation for its eventual economic transformation, and Sher Shah Suri who built the Grand Trunk Road in India – although both had their lives cut short and their foundational work was completed by their successors.

On the longer side, it should be noted that it can take even several years or decades for social causes to take hold – Mahatma Gandhi, Nelson Mandela, Martin Luther King, Ralph Nader – all needed more than 15 years to impact their communities with their respective life-transforming philosophies or ideologies.

For a country like India, the road ahead to achieving prosperity is long as explained in detail by Vijay Joshi in a recent book. The author suggests that it will take 15 years of growth at 7% for India to reach high-income country status as per current UN criteria, and possibly a generation, say 25 to 30 years, to achieve prosperity similar to that of Portugal today.

Should India not wait patiently for another 30 years then? After all, India has made substantial progress in the 70 years since independence, such that it is viewed as a rising power all over the world, so why not 30 years more? The answer lies in the "window of opportunity" that will close demographically and new competition that is bound to come from other emerging countries like Brazil, Indonesia, and eventually Africa.

In addition to time and continuity, there is the issue of leadership. The impact leaders have depends on their leadership skills and the time they have to leave their imprint. They should have an empowering vision that attracts their followers, a clear strategy, expert execution skills to achieve their visions, and the ability to stay in power long enough to realize their visions. In the absence of any of these factors, they are likely to fall short of their potential. The three traits of any great leader are passion, compassion, and competence. If any of these sterling qualities is absent, it is impossible to either win over or attract loyal followers or achieve the credibility/ability to realize their visions.

Considerable research has gone into what makes a good leader and the different types of leadership and even though there is no formula as such for determining the effectiveness of a leader, considerable empirical data exists as to how long it takes for a leader to make a minor impact, a major impact, or to achieve a complete transformation of their institutions or countries.

Chapter 2

Types of Leaders, Their Mission Orientations, and Tasks

Leadership research suggests that three different styles of leadership exist: Situational, Transactional, and Transformational. Leaders tend to follow one or the other style according to their beliefs and instincts. It is always possible for leaders to adopt different leadership styles depending on the situation, their pragmatism, or survival instincts as they progress through their careers but it is rare.

The characteristics of these three types of leaders, their orientations, and key tasks are summarized in the table below, followed by a detailed discussion.

Table 2.1	Types of leaders, their mission orientation, and tasks		
	Situational	**Transactional**	**Transformational**
Mission	Organize	Mutual Exchange	Change/Innovation
Focus	Short-term	Maintain status quo	Long-term
Tasks	a. Structure	a. Contractual relations	a. Vision
	b. Communication	b. Compromise	b. Reforms
	c. Instructions	c. Benefits	c. Strategy/ Tactics

Situational leadership can be task- or people-oriented and can be exercised in a democratic, autocratic, or laissez-faire manner. A task-oriented leader gives clear instructions, creates organizational structures, and establishes formal communication channels. A people-oriented leader is more concerned about maintaining harmonious relationships, reducing emotional conflicts, and ensuring equal participation. In either case, the focus is short-term and the priority is to manage the situation at hand. Such leaders can successfully manage difficult, complex situations within a short time or specified timeframe. Some well-known examples of situational leaders who had successfully managed various types of complex situations include: Lenin during the Russian Revolution after the abdication of Tsar Nicholas II (the last Emperor of Russia), turning the situation to Bolshevik advantage (the Bolshevik Party was later renamed as the Communist Party of the Soviet Union); Winston Churchill taking over from Neville Chamberlain during World War II leading to the Allies victory; Nelson Mandela ending apartheid after his release from prison and eventually voted in 1994 as the first black president of South Africa; Sardar Patel integrating India through the accession of princes ruling Indian states; and P.V. Narasimha Rao's economic reforms after India's Balance of Payments (BoP) crisis in 1991. However, while managing complicated circumstances is critical, nation-building is a much more onerous task since it has many dimensions of social, cultural, and economic change, takes much more time, and faces greater overt/covert opposition.

Transactional leadership is based on mutual exchanges between leaders and their followers. Such leaders accomplish their objectives by motivating their followers by offering implicit or explicit contracts aimed at mutual gains, or through compromises that seek to protect the interests of all parties concerned. Such leaders can exercise power for a long time but their ideological stance or instincts are not conducive to producing major changes in the polity. Difficult decisions are not taken or they are postponed and the long-term consequences of short-term actions are seldom taken into account, as long as the benefits accrue to the leaders and/or their followers. Some examples of transactional leaders are Lyndon Johnson in the United States, and Charles De Gaulle in France, both of whom pushed through major reforms when circumstances put them at their countries' helm of affairs. In a similar vein, the Allied leadership during World War II put aside major ideological differences to forge a common front for winning the war.

In the Indian context, the best examples of transactional leaders are Indira and Rajiv Gandhi; they both had their successes as well as major failures, and neither of them thought about the long-range consequences of their actions that made the institutional framework weaker while their Congress

Party's ideology and ideals reigned supreme. At the same time, Indira Gandhi led India through a difficult period and deserves credit for the Green Revolution and successful resolution of the Bangladesh crisis, while Rajiv Gandhi initiated India's halting first steps towards economic reform as well as embraced the emerging digital technology.

Transformational leaders are almost always charismatic, able to articulate an inspiring vision, and show a path toward achieving their vision. They can raise their followers' level of consciousness about the importance and values of the desired outcomes. Such leaders show enthusiasm and optimism, do not compromise easily, and exercise idealized influence and inspirational motivation among their followers. The followers attribute their leaders with qualities they wish to emulate and are impressed with their behaviors. The intellectual stimulation caused by such leaders to engage their followers in innovative efforts to change old ways of thinking and existing frameworks, embrace reform, and take on ever more challenging goals is worth recognizing. Such leaders are always pragmatic and their charisma and massive followership enable them to forge win/win solutions among conflicting stakeholders. They tend to stay above the day-to-day back and forth between warring factions among their own followers as well as the opposition.

Transformational leaders give priority to long-range choices even at the expense of short-term popularity. India has been fortunate to have several such transformational leaders: from Mahatma Gandhi and Sardar Patel to Jawaharlal Nehru – all these great leaders certainly belong in this pantheon. And while it may be too early to say, in Narendra Modi, India may have found another transformational leader as we will discuss later in this book. Modi sees himself as a transformational leader and has called for his government to *"reform, perform, transform"* and his supporters believe that the foundation for India's transformation has been laid during his first term (2014-19).

The most obvious question is: how long do these leaders need to be in power to make a widespread impact? History suggests that while it is possible to make a far-reaching impact in five years (think Sher Shah Suri or Narasimha Rao), or a major impact in eight to ten years (like many Presidents of the United States), more time is needed to achieve a complete transformation (such as that achieved by Deng Xiaoping in China or Ataturk in Turkey). Going by even more examples such as that of Napoleon, Bismarck, Caesar, or Alexander, it appears that around 15 years is the average length of time required to successfully guide a nation towards attaining tangible growth.

Both Deng Xiaoping (in power from 1978-92 in China) and Kemal Ataturk (1923-38 in Turkey) were able to transform their countries through their leadership within 15 years. China started its climb to superpower status and Turkey its social transformation because of its leadership and execution skills. Other examples that come to mind are Napoleon (1799-1814), Bismarck (1871-90), Caesar (59-44 BCE), and Alexander (36-23 BCE). It is clear that all transformational leaders unequivocally average around 15 years. Obviously, it is not a rigid formula, but around 15 years seems to be the "gestation period" needed for ground-breaking transformational accomplishments.

Our proposition in this book is that for India to become a superpower, it requires a transformational leader at the helm for a sufficiently long period. In the next chapter, we will review examples of nation-building for all kinds of nations, large to small, homogeneous to heterogeneous, from Europe to Asia, followed by what is meant by superpower status, and the likelihood that in Modi, India has possibly got the transformational leader capable of taking it to that esteemed goal.

It is not sufficient to only talk effusively about leadership without mentioning that the followers' attitudes and the support they get from them matter a lot too. The saying that *no man is an island* rightly fits in this circumstance. For a leader to do an exceedingly great job, he must have reliable, dedicated, and ever-ready followers who are willing to go the extra mile in making sure his policies work and his socioeconomic projects are properly and timely executed.

Several studies have been conducted on the subject of "followership" and there are intrinsically two theoretical followership approaches: **the role-based approach** and the **constructionalist approach.** Let's critically analyze each category of these followership principles as follows:

I.   **Role-based Approach:** This is also referred to as the **"reversing-the-lens"** approach. As shown in Figure 2.1 below, the role-based approach investigates the effects of followers' characteristics/behaviors on the leaders' overall actions/behaviors. In other words, a leader may be transformational and ready and willing to cause good, seismic, or earthshaking transformations in his country but if his followers' attitudes to change or development are lukewarm and unsupportive, that leader will only end up being frustrated and burned out. It is a fact that there is no true leadership when there are no supportive followers.

| Figure 2.1 | Role-based approach followership |

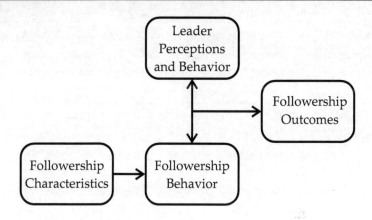

Source: PennState Leadership Blog

Concerning followership characteristics/behaviors, it is important to consider which attitudes may be considered supportive or not. Table 2.2 provides a clear picture of what is expected of supportive followers.

| Table 2.2 | Difference between supportive and unsupportive followers |

Responsibility	Supportive Followership	Unsupportive Followership
Legal	Obeys all the laws	Mostly disobeys legal authorities or chooses to obey the laws that only serve their purposes
Orderliness	Well-behaved, is always considerate about others' feelings and actions	Chaotic, always on the edge of committing violent acts

Responsibility	Supportive Followership	Unsupportive Followership
Social responsibility	Puts the society/community first, and works towards building up their societies	Causes chaos, disharmony, and confusion in their societies/communities
Political responsibility	Peacefully exercises their voting rights or suffrage and is always willing to support good and credible political candidates	Never participates in any voting activities and may debar others from exercising their voting rights or suffrage
Fiscal responsibility	Regularly pays their taxes and financially supports their government in any way they can	Avoids paying taxes and are consistently unconcerned about their government's financial needs
General support	Wants their countries to be the best in the world and offers maximum support for the government-in-power	Does not care about showing any support to their governments

From the foregoing, it is apparent that any leader's success in power directly depends on whether their followers are supportive or unsupportive.

II. **Constructionalist Approach:** On the other hand, the constructionalist theory of followership, which is also called the **"relational-based"** approach reveals how the relationship between a leader and his followers could make or mar the followership outcomes. This entails that when there is a robust relationship between a leader and those who follow him, this may lead to mutually beneficial outcomes, short-term or long-term, depending on how long the rapport or comradeship is maintained.

This explains why sometimes when political parties form an alliance to govern a nation, the chief actors or those who are elected to senior positions in the alliance must always be on the same page and maintain good relationships with one another in order to advance the causes or missions of the alliance. On the contrary, any unsettled differences or rancor can easily pull the alliance apart.

Figure 2.2 **Constructionalist approach of followership**

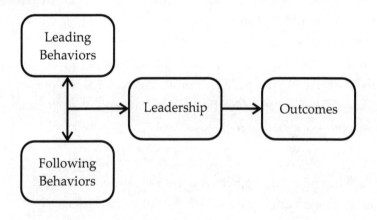

Source: PennState Leadership Blog

In principle, followers first of all size up their leaders and their behaviors and decide if they are worth throwing their absolute support behind or not. This is where a leader's credibility comes into full play; a corrupt leader may force himself into power, but he cannot compel people to follow him.

By all measures, followers are much more excited to follow leaders who show them how to do a thing rather than tell them to do it without participating in it themselves. The reason why Mahatma Gandhi is called the Father of India is that instead of just sitting comfortably in his house and telling people what to do to drive the British colonizers from India and demand independence for their beloved country, he put himself on the line and marched ahead of the people during organized peaceful protests. Followers can readily identify genuineness in their leaders, and when they see someone who is not self-engrossed and manipulative, they willingly forget about themselves and do whatever such leaders urge them to do. The same cult-like followership can be said of Martin Luther King Jr., who mobilized African-Americans to fight for their constitutional rights in the United States, even when such a brazen act could cost him his dear life, as it eventually did. The transactionalist theory of followership indicates that a deep-seated relationship between leaders and their ardent followers will be built over the course of time, and that bond alone could make leadership easier for those voted into political positions or appointed to lead.

On the contrary, the elitist tendency seen in Indian politics makes the relationship between modern Indian leaders and their followers appear more like that of a role-based type. Nowadays, Indian politicians are fond of demonstrating an if-you-rub-my-palm-I-would-rub-your-back kind of relationship with their followers. This can be blamed on extreme regionalism and casteism that are still prevalent in some communities, regions, and states in India. When in power, regional leaders tend to focus on developing their regions, a practice that could increase tension in the polity when certain areas of the country are neglected and not carried along in the national development.

Prime Minister Modi has proved that his agendas are national and for every Indian citizen, and that might explain why he was considered to be the most popular leader in the world with an approval rating of 71% in 2022, beating America's Joe Biden (43%), Canada's Justin Trudeau (43%), and Japan's Fumio Kishida (48%). Even though these were simply survey results, they indicated that the world has been closely following or monitoring Modi's unprecedented efforts at transforming the Indian economy in all its ramifications.

What could cause followers to desert their leaders and eventually cripple their policies, no matter how grand they seem to be? The demise of the USSR offers the obvious reason why leaders could lose their followers within a short period, even if such followers were previously loyal and had been diehard or fanatic supporters. The 15 republics that comprised the former USSR were at the crossroads of determining their national identities – they knew they were not ethnic Russians, and every effort to make them assume they were by the eight de facto rulers of the old USSR (who were all Russians) failed woefully. More so, the centrally controlled socioeconomic policies of the Soviet era did not favor those 14 other republics, as their people were mired in abject poverty and suffering from intense hunger.

Followers, like a river, flow in the direction that favors them. What makes India remain as divided as it is today is that some past political leaders in the country have been able, through their divisive policies, to draw certain kinds of followers to themselves. However, if we are to grow as a nation, we must embrace unity in all its forms; a feat that could only be achieved by a transformative leader who has the interest of India at heart – a leadership characteristic already noticeable in Prime Minister Modi.

This page is intentionally left blank

Chapter 3

Historical Perspectives: Some Examples of Successful National Transformations

Let's consider some examples of nation-building, of countries large and small, with diverse or homogeneous populations, in Europe, America, and Asia, during the past century. There are many more examples in history than those discussed in this book, but the most relevant ones are those that happened during the Industrial Age, most especially when nations underwent a structural transformation during a long period under the leadership of one leader. The examples included in this discussion are Turkey under the leadership of Mustafa Kemal Ataturk, the United States under Franklin Delano Roosevelt, Germany under Konrad Adenauer after World War II and then again under Helmut Kohl, Singapore under Lee Kuan Yew, South Korea under Park Chung Hee, Taiwan under Lee Teng Hui, and China under Deng Xiaoping. Additionally, we discuss a current example of nation-building in progress – India.

World War I heralded the beginning of the end of colonialism and colonial powers. The United States became the dominant power in the world and the next hundred years were very much an American century. While the colonial powers carried on for another generation, and it was not until the end of World War II that they were finally exhausted, other nations began to emerge, some successfully and others haltingly.

The very first nation to rebuild itself was Turkey, under the transformative leadership of Mustafa Kemal, better known as Ataturk or father of the Turks. The Ottoman Empire had seen sporadic efforts at reform, starting with Sultan Abdul Hamid II and subsequently during the July 1908 "Young Turks" Revolution, which competed Abdul Hamid II (the last sultan of the unified Turkey) to restore the Ottoman Constitution, but none had succeeded. Indeed, Turkey faced complete chaos and dismemberment after its defeat in World War I, the Ottoman Empire being one of the losing troika of central powers along with the German and Austro-Hungarian empires. Out of the ashes of defeat arose Mustafa Kemal, who formidably managed to preserve the Turkish nation, even as the Kurdish, Greek, and Arab parts of the Ottoman Empire were lost. Having secured Turkey to its current borders during the post-war years (1919-1923), the monarchy (Caliphate) was abolished in favor of a Western-styled republic and Mustafa Kemal became its first President. Over the next 15 years, he proceeded on a campaign of nation-building and initiated a series of political, legal, religious, cultural, social, and economic reforms that transformed Turkey from an Islamist monarchy to a modern, secular nation, for which he was hailed as Ataturk by his people.

What transpired in Turkey was a transformation in its truest sense. The dress was Westernized, Latin script was adopted setting aside the Arabic-Persian script, secularism became the state policy, and the power of the clergy was curtailed. The capital was shifted from Istanbul to Ankara, and state-driven five-year-development plans were initiated. Even though Turkey has never been a classical liberal democracy, its policies were defined as Kemalist with the military having a major role in the country's direction and policies. Mustafa Kemal was a field marshal himself in the Turkish military who actively participated in some military offensives such as the Italo-Turkish War (1911-1912), the Balkan Wars (1912-1913), and World War I, defending the unity of Turkey. To this day, Turkey remains one of the few democracies in the Muslim world where elections are held regularly, individual freedoms are permitted (within limits), with a free market economy linked to the global economy.

The United States is another example of remarkable, national rejuvenation under the "New Deal" programs of Franklin Delano Roosevelt, culminating in victory in World War II. After the stock market collapse in 1929, followed by the decade-long Great Depression (1929-1939) that Americans experienced, an atmosphere of despair existed when Roosevelt took charge in 1933. After first inspiring his fellow citizens with his admonition that *"we have nothing to fear except fear itself…"* Roosevelt embarked on a bold policy of state intervention with public works providing employment opportunities while building the infrastructure. New laws were promulgated for banking and financial institutions' reform to prevent a repeat of reckless investing that had led to the 1929 Stock Market Crash when people borrowed money excessively to purchase stocks on speculation and used huge leverage in the process. Their audacious but risky investing practices caused the value of the Dow Jones Industrial Average to decline by 13% on October 28, 1929, which is popularly referred to as the "Black

Monday". Major new construction projects were undertaken
by the Roosevelt administration such as the Grand Coulee
Dam on the Columbia River and the development of Tennessee
Valley, expanding electricity and farming operations across
huge swaths of territories in a dedicated effort to jumpstart
the American economy. Slowly the economy revived, public
confidence was restored, and Roosevelt was not only re-elected
but went on to lead the United States for an unprecedented
four terms. After his death at the beginning of his fourth term,
Vice President Harry Truman carried on his policies, thus
maintaining continuity.

Germany was prostrate and economically weakened
after its defeat in World War II, structurally divided into
four zones. The zones under the occupation of the United
States, United Kingdom, and France came together to form
West Germany – a liberal democracy, while the Soviet
Union-occupied zone became East Germany, its communist
satellite. Konrad Adenauer became West Germany's de facto
leader as its Chancellor and remained in power for 14 years
(1949-63). During this period, West Germany underwent an
extraordinary recovery helped by the United States through
the $17.6 billion Marshall Plan or European Recovery Program
aimed at reviving Western Europe. This recovery called the
"German miracle" resulted in democracy growing deep roots
and fundamental changes in Germany's outlook towards its
former enemies, eventually resulting in the "Treaty of Rome"
that established a common market of six countries (Germany,
France, Italy, Belgium, Netherlands, and Luxembourg) in
1957. West Germany again became an economic giant, and
the idea of a United States of Europe took hold. Subsequent
developments have seen the evolution of this common market

into the European Economic Community and finally into the European Union of today.

Another nation-building opportunity for Germany arose after the collapse of the Soviet Union under the leadership of Helmut Kohl (1982-98). After the demise of the Soviet Union, the burning issue then was the way forward for its satellite nations, one of which was East Germany. Kohl seized the opportunity by first getting the Western powers to agree not to expand NATO (that they reneged on this in later years is another matter) and then mandating equal exchange rate of the two currencies of West and East Germany, as was desired by East Germany. The equal exchange rate policy was politically necessary but economically disastrous – it led to economic difficulties for the West Germans due to the differences in productivity between the two countries. Inflation increased, fiscal policies required additional taxation, and eventually, Kohl's party lost elections. Kohl was out of power but he had achieved the transformation of Germany because much of its historical territory had been restored before his ouster. Since then the additional population and economic power of the United Germany has ensured its primacy in Europe!

Singapore was an island outpost under the British with a diverse population of Chinese, Malays, and Indians. After independence in 1959, Lee Kuan Yew became Prime Minister of Singapore and continued in that role until 1990 which, at the time, made him the longest-serving PM in the world! He supported Tengku Abdul Rehman's proposal to form Malaysia comprising a union of Malaya, Singapore, Sabah, and Sarawak in 1963. However, due to ideological and economic differences that resulted in riots between the Malays and the Chinese, Singapore was unceremoniously forced out of the Union and became an independent republic on August 9, 1965. Even though Lee Kuan Yew considered it a grave injustice and was greatly distressed initially to the point of being in tears when he announced the imminent separation from Malaysia, he put this event behind him and set out to build Singapore as a prosperous city-state.

Lee Kuan Yew favored long-term social and economic planning, macroeconomic stability, social harmony, and discipline for managing the diverse population of Singapore. Even though unemployment was high in the initial years, he eschewed populist policies and ensured a budget surplus with a stable currency. He sought to make Singapore a financial center and attract multinationals. Initially focused on manufacturing, with electronics exports as the priority, he opened up new sectors of the knowledge economy, from airlines and banking to tourism. Infrastructure was built and global linkages were created to attract multinational companies, both to encourage them to situate their full operations as well as set up regional headquarters in Singapore. Additionally, he introduced conscription for Singapore's defense and encouraged close cooperation with other "small" countries like Israel and Taiwan. His foreign policy took Singapore into the United Nations. Singapore was a founding member of ASEAN in 1967, along with four other Southeast Asian nations, namely Malaysia, Thailand, Indonesia, and the Philippines.

Lee Kuan Yew kept a firm grip on power, with strict media control and curtailed civil liberties that might have probably ensured the continuity of his government. Meritocracy was encouraged with the public sector's salaries at par with the private sector's wages. Corruption was rooted out, yet the "ease of doing business" could not have been easier, even at a time when the World Bank was not even measuring such metrics! Additionally, social harmony was ensured by making sure that every neighborhood had a Chinese, Indian, and Malay presence. Civic discipline was promoted through strict laws, sometimes judged by critics to be far too autocratic, but they worked and over time changed Singaporeans' social behaviors. Health, education, and vocational training were given priority to upgrade the skills of the population.

Sustained national revitalization efforts during the period of Lee Kuan Yew's leadership produced impressive results that could not have been more dramatic. Singapore went from the third world to the first world within the span of one generation. Between 1960 and 2022, Singapore's per capita GDP rose to $82,808 from $428 (1960), unemployment dropped from 4.85% (1999) to 2.76% (2022), external trade rose to $870.81 billion (2022) from $1.5 billion (1960), life expectancy at birth went to 84 (2022) from 65 (1960), literacy rate to 97.13% (2022) from 82.9% (1980), and tourist arrivals went from a miniscule 99,000 (1965) to 19.1 million (2019).

Lee Kuan Yew's policies have continued under his handpicked successors. Today, Singapore's GDP is $466.79 billion (nominal) (2022) or $719 billion (PPP) (2022); per capita GDP is $82,808 (nominal) (2022) or $108,036 (PPP) – higher than that of the United States, and its foreign trade exceeds $870.81 billion (2022) – approaching twice its GDP. Though many had doubted the viability of Singapore at the start, it not only went on to become one of the "Asian Tigers" alongside Hong Kong, South Korea, and Taiwan but also is now ahead of most of the 34 developed countries included in the OECD (Organization of Economic Cooperation and Development). Lee Kuan

Yew, with his peculiar achievements in nation-building, has influenced other countries as well, notably China after Deng Xiaoping visited Singapore and emulated its economic policies, encouraging entrepreneurship, and engaging in subtle suppression of dissidents. Both India and Russia have tried to emulate Singapore with varying degrees of success.

South Korea went through a similar transformation under Park Chung Hee, although through a much more autocratic process – essentially dictatorial with striking similarities to Turkey's Ataturk's approach. Park Chung Hee came to power through a military coup on May 16, 1961, assumed the presidency in 1963, and stayed in control of Korea until his assassination in 1979. He was greatly influenced by Germany and Japan having worked for the Japanese during World War II and believed that autocratic means were needed to bring about national reconstruction. He has been criticized for his dictatorial policies, although most South Koreans regard him as their greatest president.

During the 18 years of Park Chung Hee's reign, South Korea underwent rapid economic growth with an export-oriented industrialization policy similar to that of Japan – albeit with some differences: five year plans on the Soviet Union / China / India model, which involved state encouragement of conglomerates like LG, Samsung, Hyundai with incentives and cheap loans. At the same time, 24-hour electricity was provided to every village, roads were built to link every village to urban centers, and thatched roofs were replaced with tin roofs. The use of "Hanja" or "Hancha" Chinese characters was abolished in favor of the Korean "Hangul" script, and metrification of measures replaced Korean measures to ensure consistency with international norms and standards.

After Park Chung Hee, his successors continued his economic policies while democratizing the South Korean political system. The results have been as astounding as in Singapore; South Korea's GDP was a mere $2.42 billion in 1961 with a per capita GDP of about $100. When Park came to power; it rose to $246 billion in 1989, and since then it has risen to $1623.90 billion (2017) with a per capita income of about $31,617 (nominal) or $ 41,001 (PPP). South Korean foreign trade exceeded $1 trillion in 2021.

In contrast, India's GDP in 2019 was $2850 billion, per capita income of $2134 (nominal) or $7783 (PPP) and foreign trade of $768 billion, even though India has 32 times the land area and 25 times the population and was ahead of South Korea in every metric at the time Park came to power in 1961.

Taiwan, being an island separated from mainland China, became a separate entity under Chiang Kai Shek (also called Jiang Zhongzheng or Jiang Jieshi) after his defeat by the communists under Mao in 1949. The early years were needed for stabilization following which Taiwan began to industrialize with some assistance from the United States. While Chiang's rule was autocratic, democratic reforms began under his son, Lee Teng Hui (1975-88). Taiwanese economic policies were similar to the export-led manufacturing policies adopted by South Korea. Starting with the establishment of Hsinchu Science Park on December 15, 1980, today there are six such industrial parks – each comprising a cluster of industries and a hub for start-ups.

Taiwan is about the size of Kerala with a population of about 24 million; however, its GDP is $206.1 billion (nominal) (2022) or $761 billion (PPP), per capita of $32,756 (nominal) or $35,510 (PPP) (2022). The total foreign trade is $907 billion (2022) or nearly the same as its GDP PPP, in contrast to India's 27%. And that is when India has made impressive strides since reforms in 1991 at which time it was only 7%.

Chapter 4

India's Laudable Dance Towards Significant National Transformation: Comparing India to China

Let us now turn to China, similar in size (in terms of arable land even though China is nearly three times in geographic area) and population to India but with a different political system. After the upheavals of the Mao era, China was comparable to India in terms of its GDP, per capita GDP, and human development indices (though with a higher literacy rate) when Deng Xiaoping began his reforms in 1978. Beginning with agricultural reforms, he adopted the Singaporean model by creating Special Export Zones (SEZ) that manufactured goods primarily earmarked for export with infrastructure to facilitate entrepreneurship and attract multinational companies. Private property was allowed, contracts enforced, and people were duly encouraged to engage in profitable economic activities (*to be rich is glorious*! said Deng Xiaoping to his people).

Political dogma was abandoned in favor of pragmatism (Deng silenced ideological opposition to his policies through his most famous quote *"It does not matter if the cat is black*

or white, as long as it catches mice". The new system was
called "Socialism with Chinese characteristics" to mollify
conservatives and overcome the resistance that raised its head
from time to time. At the same time, the single-party system
under the communists continued, people with dissenting
opinions were stifled, and democracy was discouraged. Deng
stayed in power during 1978-92 and continued in advisory
roles until he died in 1997 at the age of 93.

China's economic progress since 1980 has been nothing
short of astonishing and must be acknowledged as such. Its
GDP rose from about $300 billion (both in nominal and PPP
terms) in 1989 to about $426.92 billion (nominal) and $1469
billion (PPP) in 1992. During the 2000s, China surpassed Italy,
France, the UK, and Germany in turn until it became the
second-largest economy in nominal terms after overtaking
Japan in 2010. In PPP terms, China had already become the
second-largest economy in 1999 surpassing Japan, and became
the largest world economy in 2014 catching up with the United
States. Today, the Chinese economy is nearly 3/4th of the
United States' nominal terms and far ahead in PPP ($30,327
billion as compared to the US' $22,993 billion (2021)). Of course,
given it is four times as large in population, China is still far
behind when it comes to the prosperity of its people: per capita
GDP being $11,560 (2022) as compared to $62,867 (2022) for the
United States. Nonetheless, the day is not too far when China
emerges as the world's largest economy and the prosperity of
its people approaches that of advanced nations like those in the
OECD.

India achieved independence on August 15, 1947, virtually
around the same time as the communist takeover of China
on October 1, 1949. Its economic history since then can be

characterized as consisting of four distinct phases. The first phase is the Nehru years of hope and disillusion (1947-64) with socialism, neutrality, and self sufficiency (resulting in one of the most closed economies in the world) as dominant ideologies. The second phase is the period from 1964-80. Nehru's policies were not only followed by his ideological successors – Lal Bahadur Shastri and Indira Gandhi's first term (1964-66 and 1966-77)– but also the country turned even more socialistic with lower growth rates. The third phase is the period during 1980-91 with some opening up of the economy during Indira Gandhi's second term and emphasis on economic growth through fiscal spending expansion during the Rajiv Gandhi years (1964-89). However, the resultant fiscal overspending led to a BoP crisis in 1991, at which time the astute new PM, P.V. Narasimha Rao, along with his Finance Minister Manmohan Singh, pushed through reforms abolishing most stringent governmental controls and opening up the economy to foreign investments, multinational companies, and international trade.

While India muddled through the first three phases, other countries determinedly passed it by; for example, Japan recovered rapidly from its devastation in World War II, then the miraculous rise of the "Asian Tigers" consisting of Taiwan, South Korea, Hong Kong, and Singapore, and finally the birth of modern and progressive China! While it was possible to rationalize that Japan's economic miracle was largely due to its pre-war industrialization and post-war American help, the peculiar rise of "Asian Tigers" may be considered irrelevant as these were small economies. However, it was not possible to ignore the rise of China – a country even larger than India that had lagged behind India within living memory.

China had abandoned its communist collectivist policies in favor of free-market trade-oriented policies following Deng Xiaoping's rise to power in 1978 and began to grow at rates similar to that of the "Asian Tigers" during the 1980s. While this did not go unnoticed in India, there were very few visionaries in the political establishment that had the courage or credibility to challenge established political orthodoxies, and so India remained somnolent until the economic crisis of 1991 that left it with no apparent option except to seek an IMF bailout and carry out the economic reforms mandated by the international financial institution. India then adopted free-market policies, demolished the "License Raj" that was throttling its entrepreneurial spirits, devalued its currency, and abandoned its protectionist policies in favor of integration with the rapidly globalizing world.

The reform process initiated by the Narasimha Rao/ Manmohan Singh duo accelerated during the subsequent governments, especially the Atal Bihari Vajpayee BJP-led center-right NDA (National Democratic Alliance) coalitions of 1998-2004; it continued even with the center-left Congress-led UPA (United Progressive Alliance) coalition that came after 2004 and had a successful term through 2009. However, once the electorate rewarded the UPA coalition with another term in 2009, things seemed to go out of control until India was once more faced with an impending BoP crisis in 2013 when it began to be referred to as one of the five fragile major economies of the world.

Fortunately for India, a two-party system has evolved as its democracy matures, even though there is a plethora of regional parties with regional leaders along with the usual extremes of the left or the right. Thus, when the failings of the Congress-led

UPA became too obvious, the electorate turned to the BJP-led NDA in 2014. Moreover, the grassroots' push for younger and more dynamic leadership brought Modi to the fore, and proved his credentials through three terms (2001-14) as Gujarat Chief Minister even though some questioned his credentials due to the unfortunate riots at the very beginning of his term in 2002.

Since 2014, Modi has led India successfully with major reforms and increased its influence across the world. India is now the fastest-growing economy in the world – the third overall in terms of Purchasing Power Parity (PPP) and sixth in nominal dollar terms. And so India continues on its transformative economic trajectory regardless of which party is in power, albeit with some differences arising from the center-right or center-left orientation of its ruling dispensation.

Let us now compare China to India on their separate economic journeys. China initiated reforms and opened up its economy in 1978 while India did so in 1991. The first question is how far have their economies performed since reforms, both chronologically and on a time-adjusted "normalized" basis, which takes into account their different starting points? Table 4.1 shows their overall GDP growths in both nominal and purchasing power terms at the times their distinctive reforms were initiated and 27 years after the reforms (1991-2018) to gauge how far each economy grew during the same time period after the start.

Table 4.1	\ GDP comparison of China and India – nominal dollar basis ($ Billion)					
	1978	**1991**	**2005**	**2018**	**2020**	**2022**
CHINA	218	380	2,287	1,3457	15,462	17,963
INDIA	140	278	834	2,690	3,258	3,530

Source: IMF data

On a purchasing power parity (PPP) basis, which arguably is a better reflection of the relative size of an economy, India has grown even faster when compared with the growth of China and India 27 years after reforms were initiated in 1978 and 1991 respectively (Chinese economy in 2005 compared to India in 2018).

Table 4.2	\ GDP comparison of China and India – Purchasing Power Parity basis ($ Billion)					
	1978	**1991**	**2005**	**2018**	**2020**	**2022**
CHINA	305	1,264	6,552	25,313	29,712	36,100
INDIA	381	1,030	3,238	10,401	12,531	11,400

Source: IMF data

So, how prosperous is the average Chinese person as compared to an Indian? For this, we turn to GDP on a per capita basis, as shown in the table below. Even by this metric India has done better than China 27 years after initiating reforms (comparing India's GDP per capita in 2018 to China's in 2015).

Table 4.3	GDP per capita comparison of China and India					
	1980	**1991**	**2005**	**2018**	**2020**	**2022**
CHINA-NOMINAL ($)	310	358	1,765	9,633	10,970	12.813
CHINA-PPP ($)	310	1,095	5,064	18,120	21.080	21,392
INDIA-NOMINAL ($)	276	318	747	2,016	2,370	2,379
INDIA-PPP ($)	559	1,198	2,902	7,795	9,150	8,329

Source: IMF data

Another metric for measuring the wellbeing of people is the Human Development Index (HDI) which includes per capita income, income inequality, education, and life expectancy. Countries are grouped into four categories according to their HDIs: very high, high, medium, and low. Both China and India have made unprecedented progress and have ranked 86 and 130 currently among the 189 countries in the 2017 rankings. Until recently both countries were in the medium

HDI group; only recently China has moved up to the high HDI group, which has a cut-off of .75. The steadily upwards trend line for both countries is shown in Table 4.4.

Table 4.4	Human Development Index (HDI) trends – India and China								
	1990	**2000**	**2010**	**2012**	**2014**	**2015**	**2016**	**2017**	**2022**
INDIA	0.427	0.493	0.581	0.60	0.618	0.627	0.636	0.64	0.633
CHINA	0.502	0.594	0.706	0.722	0.738	0.743	0.748	0.748	0.768

Source: UNDP human development reports

So how far ahead is China's economy and the prosperity of its citizens as compared to India?

The short answer is: not very far, about a decade or so! India being behind should not come as a surprise; after all, India gave up its socialist ethos 13 years after China. That can translate to a fourfold difference at the 10% growth rate that China was able to achieve at its peak rates of growth. The surprise is that India's raucous democracy has done relatively well compared to China's autocratic political system.

During the last decade, the world has paid much more attention to China's growing economy due to its larger absolute size and highest contribution to incremental growth in the global GDP. China became the largest economy in the world in PPP terms in 2014 overtaking the United States and is expected to become so in nominal terms as well within the next five years. While India has not garnered as much attention as China, it became the third-largest economy in PPP terms at the beginning of this decade, and it moved up to the sixth-largest in nominal terms during the last five years. India surpassed the UK this year (2023) to become the fifth-largest economy in nominal dollar terms. If the current level of growth is sustained, India is expected to become fourth by 2025 overtaking Germany, and third by 2030 overtaking Japan. While projections beyond 2030 are much less reliable, India will certainly be among the new "triad" of economic powers after 2030.

The growth of the Indian economy in recent years, as well as its trajectory, as compared to other major Western economies and Japan is shown in Table 4.5.

Table 4.5	Comparison of the Indian economy to that of Japan and leading European nations (Nominal $ basis; $ Billion)						
	2017	2018	2019	2020	2021	2022	2023
Japan	4,872	5,167	5,362	5,498	5,641	5,796	5,962
Germany	3,684	4,211	4,416	4,628	4,837	5,055	5,727
UK	2,624	2,936	3,022	3,121	3,227	3,350	3,476
France	2,583	2,925	3,060	3,196	3,324	3,457	3,585
India	2,611	2,848	3,155	3,477	3,832	4,226	4,663

Source: IMF data

Finally, it should be noted that while we have focused on nation-building during the past century as it is most relevant to the present – given the socioeconomic, geopolitical, and technological context, earlier examples from the 19th century, such as that of Germany under Bismarck, Japan during the Meiji restoration, Italy under Cavour, France under Napoleon, indicate similar outcomes. Thus, national transformation requires considerable time, continuity, steadfastness of vision, and transformational (charismatic but pragmatic) leadership. Even if we were to look earlier than that in history, when nation-states did not exist and monarchy was the prevalent system, the same is true: from the West to the East, from Alexander to Caesar, from Ashoka to Harsha, from Genghis Khan to Akbar.

In the next chapter, we turn to what lessons can be drawn from history. What types of economic and political systems are the necessary conditions for success? How long is the journey and what types of leaders are needed?

This page is intentionally left blank

Chapter 5

Lessons Learned from History: How and When Transformation Occurs

In this chapter, we review key lessons from history, taking into consideration the necessary and sufficient conditions for national transformation and highlighting the peculiar characteristics of leaders who have succeeded at this enormous task.

The necessary but not sufficient conditions are stability of political conditions, continuity of policies, and visionary but pragmatic leadership. In addition to the necessary conditions (or the transformative prerequisites for nation-building), other factors that can be deemed as sufficient conditions are the country's infrastructure, linkages to the external world, strategies and tactics adopted for national transformation, and human and financial capital investment.

The political system must be stable, as long as the nature of the system is not chaotic and anti-progressive. Interestingly, nation-building can occur in any political system. Even though the majority of examples in the previous chapter were autocratic regimes, both the US and India have achieved appreciable levels of structural reformations as democracies.

Arguably, it may take democracies a bit longer to reach the mandatory consensus needed to move any reforms forward. Interestingly enough, India's democracy has not gotten in the way of its recorded progress, even though democratic processes can be quite messy, and it always takes longer to reach compromises and consensus when pushing any changes through the Parliament. At times, this could act as a stumbling block that might slow down any social or economic revamping.

The stability of regimes ensures continuity of policies, and it is even better if the transformational leader retains power for as long as needed to build a strong socioeconomic foundation. This is akin to the "gestation period" for any major project or enterprise to be successful.

It is understandable that when there is a sudden political regime change, which is most likely to result in a leadership change, it can cause stagnation or even regression in the existing reforms initiated by the former political party that was voted out or replaced. As an exception, only Taiwan, South Korea, and China have been able to maintain per capita income growth rates of over 7% for a period as long as 30 years despite experiencing regime changes, doubling every 10 years. Many other nations, such as Brazil, Malaysia, and Indonesia, have stumbled and experienced socioeconomic deceleration with a sudden change in leadership.

India stumbled under the center-left UPA government of Manmohan Singh (2004-2014) when the policies of the center-right NDA government of Atal Bihari Vajpayee (1998-2004) were substantially changed; inflation surged to double-digit rates, fiscal deficit and current account deficit increased, infrastructure building slowed down. The Modi government has had to correct many of these deficiencies. Still, it has not been able to reverse some of the populist policies including land acquisition and labor that require urgent reform. For instance, Prime Minister Modi's efforts to make land acquisition and approval fast, easy, and cheap for businesses that want to open factories were staunchly opposed by political parties and labor unions. They also hindered his attempts to reform the labor laws and make them flexible enough to accommodate the interests of both employers and employees. If done, the interlacing reforms would have facilitated India's push for expansive job creation and the establishment of subsidized social security coverage for the employees.

While India has regained its momentum, the dip in its growth trajectory during UPA's second term is undeniable – this is because the period was spent resolving the debt-and-insolvency problems created in the first term. Beyond stability is the need for a leader to be charismatic, have the right visions for the nation, and articulate credible strategies and tactics for achieving his visions; someone who can think "outside the box" and yet be pragmatic. All of the leaders in the examples cited in the previous chapter exhibit these qualities, with the possible exception of Deng Xiaoping who was overshadowed by Mao Tze Tung and Zhou En Lai (the first Premier of the People's Republic of China, 1954-1976) for most of his political career. However, his other qualities more than made up for his lack of charisma and he was able to steer the Chinese state away from dogmatic, communist principles and implemented Singapore-styled free-market policies.

The importance of having the "right vision" cannot be overemphasized. After all, every leader has a vision – Hitler, Stalin, and Mao certainly had a vision for their nations, but each of them brought disaster and unimaginable suffering to their populace, as well as to other countries.

Pragmatism, and not ideological rigidity, is critical for nation-building. After all, not all policies or initiatives are successful, and there will always be ample opportunities for course correction. On the other hand, Lee Kuan Yew, Park Chung Hee, and Deng Xiaoping not only had a vision for their countries but were rational enough to modify it or change course when circumstances required. All three experimented with different models of development with considerable trial and error during the course of their careers. Lee Kuan Yew took his inspiration from Hong Kong and set out to build Singapore into a financial hub at the crossroads of commerce in Southeast Asia, which in turn required linkages with the external world and made Singapore an attractive destination for multinationals with the requisite infrastructure, financial resources, and facilities. Park Chung Hee started out with state-driven, five-year plans on the Soviet model, but quickly abandoned it in favor of the market-driven capitalist system. South Korea built its infrastructure providing electricity, housing, and roads to every village; the literacy and vocational skills of its population were given the highest priority, and Japan's export-oriented manufacturing became the cornerstone for economic growth. Deng Xiaoping went even further; he first challenged the political orthodoxy of the agricultural collectives under the communist system and then followed it up with export-oriented manufacturing, drawing his inspiration from Singapore. In each of these case studies, the leaders' expectations were realistic, and they were willing to learn from others. In this approach, ideology was secondary to the implementation of successful policies!

In India's case, Nehru certainly had the charisma and a vision of a democratic, secular, and socialist India, neutral in its foreign-policy orientation. He certainly laid the foundation for India's democracy. However, his rigid commitment to Fabian socialist economic policies, and the inability of his followers to see beyond the ideological straitjacket of such policies, caused India to remain a closed economy much longer than any other country, even China. The success of Germany and Japan's export-oriented economic policies and their revival after the disaster of defeat in World War II was evident even during the Nehru years (1947-64), the rise of the "Asian Tigers" happened during the Indira Gandhi years (1966-77 and 1980-84)), yet it was only after the collapse of Soviet Union and a BoP crisis caused by India's profligate fiscal spending that India decided to change direction in 1991, starting with the dismantling of controls, derisively called the "License Permit Raj", reduction in import tariffs, and opening up of the economy under P.V. Narasimha Rao. This avalanche of reforms was closely followed by infrastructure-building and privatization of loss-making public sector enterprises under Atal Bihari Vajpayee, and India finally began to grow at rates attained by the Asian Tigers.

Even now the perceptible failure of Nehruvian policies is not fully accepted in India by the followers of the Congress Party and their political counterparts. However, the statistical data cannot be ignored, because the apparent failure of Nehruvian socialism, further aggravated by Indira Gandhi's lurch to the left in her quest for political supremacy, followed by policy reforms could be considered to have actually led to higher growth recorded in India over time. This is evident from the growth rates under different phases of India's economic policies shown in Table 5.1.

Table 5.1	India's GDP Growth Rate during different phases of political leadership

Year	GDP Growth Rate
1951-1965	3.9%
1965-1980	2.9%
1980-1993	5.2%
1993-2003	6.0%
2003-2011	8.5%
2011-2014	5.4%
2014-2022	7.0%

Source: India's Long Road, the search for prosperity by Vijay Joshi

It should be recognized that at the beginning, and during much of Nehru's era, there were certainly two competing models: the free-enterprise capitalist democratic system of the United States, and the state-controlled autocratic communist system of the Soviet Union, along with European countries leaning in either direction. Therefore, the fact that Nehru chose a mixed economy, with state control of "commanding heights" based on a socialistic pattern of society is understandable. However, by his later years, the example of Japan was already there. Both his inability to learn from the early example of Japan as well as that of his successors to learn from the later examples of Hong Kong, Singapore, Korea, and Taiwan is painful. This is where pragmatism – doing what works – not being hidebound by ideology in leadership is critical.

Integrating with the external world and emphasizing trade, instead of a closed economy, and promoting self-sufficiency are other prominent lessons to be learned from the above-mentioned examples. First, Japan, and then all the "Tiger

Economies" demonstrated this reality. Learning from these, China began its rapid growth period after opening up its economy and lowering trade barriers. Special Export Zones were created in China's coastal provinces, modeled after Singapore's, linkages were created with international supply chains, and foreign trade as well as investment was welcomed. India has also followed with the opening up of its economy and lowering trade barriers. However, India has been rather more successful in service sectors than in manufacturing due to its infrastructure limitations and lower labor productivity. In principle, the information technology-enabled services are less dependent on the physical infrastructure such as transport and port facilities, and require workers with English-language proficiency as compared to mechanical/electrical skills.

The strategies and tactics for national development should be based on a country's competitive advantage, which can be geopolitical, based on proximity to key markets, or availability of natural resources, such as minerals, water, arable land, or factors of production such as land, labor, capital, technology/ entrepreneurship. In each of the cases of nation-building cited above, success was achieved only when the strategies and tactics were based on the inherent advantages enjoyed. Both Singapore and South Korea started with five-year plans based on the Soviet model, before giving them up in favor of developmental models that took advantage of their proximity to global supply chains or export markets. South Korea made up for its deficiencies by connecting all its villages by roads, providing electricity to all, and emphasizing the acquisition of vocational skills in its education system. China took advantage of its cheap labor, created export-oriented manufacturing zones, and kept domestic consumption low to maximize investment from domestic savings. The probable reason why

China's consumption is quite low compared to its astronomical growth is that, in recent years, there has been a proportionate decline in the share of household income in China's national income, as evident in the sharp decline in investment income, wages, and government transfers.

In India's case, Nehruvian socialism meant following the Soviet model with the government controlling the "commanding heights" of the economy with priorities skewed towards capital-intensive heavy industries such as public utilities, foreign and domestic trade, and natural resources. India's markets were virtually closed and trade was neglected in favor of self-sufficiency. The net result was that India missed the first golden opportunity of taking advantage of labor-intensive export-oriented industries and technology transfer through trade and exposure to multinational companies. Scarce capital was directed towards inefficient public sector enterprises at the expense of the private sector or human resource development. Such policies resulted in a stifled "Nehruvian rate of growth", which was also characterized as the "Hindu rate of growth" as if it was the fault of Hindu Civilization and not the leaders' or government's policies that had resulted in low socioeconomic performance. Such policies were further aggravated by the populist policies of Indira Gandhi; reform and learning came too late for India and the opportunity for trade and manufacturing-led growth was squandered.

Both Nehru and Indira Gandhi were visionaries with mass followers and enviable stability and continuity during their long, political tenures (1947-64 and 1966-77 and 1980-1984 respectively). However, neither was sufficiently pragmatic –

Nehru was far too much influenced by the Fabian socialism ideology, whereas Indira Gandhi championed a populist vision of "banishing poverty" that was simply infeasible given India's policies and resources. Their lack of pragmatism, along with India's protectionist policies and insufficient resources, made any transformation impossible.

In contrast, in China, Deng Xiaoping recognized the folly of Mao's policies and turned the communist dogma on its head in favor of pragmatic policies in 1978. Even though the handwriting was clearly visible on the wall, India's politicians, both Congress and the Janata coalition, refused to comprehend this reality until the BoP crisis forced their hand in 1991. This "lag time" of 13 years is one of the primary reasons for India falling behind China in the race to prosperity.

The key ingredient that pragmatic leaders bring to the table is that they are capable of quickly identifying the practical steps required to achieve their vision, and they are fully aware that without the prompt execution of those strategies, achieving their vision would be practically impossible. Additionally, pragmatism enables the leader to stay in power long enough to reach their goals. As Machiavelli has counseled, the leader who gets too far ahead of their followers in driving the process of change risks losing their own crown!

The transformation process requires a visionary leader, dissatisfaction with the status quo, and logical steps toward achieving the vision. These non-negotiable steps are undertaken in the context of human and financial capital, integration with the world economy to facilitate investment and technology transfer, and infrastructure development. The human and financial capital investments come from a healthy, well-educated, and skilled workforce, as well as domestic savings while the foreign-direct investment comes from other nations. In each of the growing Asian economies, significant emphasis was placed on health and education and markets were open to foreign investments, even if these were aimed at boosting exports or encouraging technology transfer. Singapore was the first to implement policies aimed at its population becoming a key resource to attract multinational companies, in addition to its strategic location, connectivity with the necessary supply chains, and incentive tax policies. South Korea also invested in vocational skills training coupled with state support to domestic conglomerates in a way analogous to the role played by multinationals in Singapore. China and India have belatedly recognized the importance of these factors even though their other comparative advantages – labor productivity in the case of China and India's English-speaking workforce – have compensated for proportionately lower investments in human resource development as the multinational investment started to come in due to their market sizes once their doors were opened for their entry.

Chapter 6

India's Journey from Nehru to Manmohan: Socialism to Market Reforms

India achieved independence in 1947 as one of the two states carved out of British India, the other being Pakistan. In addition, there were more than 500 kingdoms and principalities dependent on the British Empire. These dependencies were given the option of acceding to India or Pakistan; some did so quickly, while others hesitated but were coerced into becoming parts of one country or the other. The one exception to this was the Kingdom of Jammu and Kashmir, which acceded to India only after being invaded by Pathan tribals with the tacit support of Pakistan that reportedly provided military support to some mujahedeen invading the Kingdom, leading to the first Indo-Pakistani War (1947-48) between the two successor states of undivided India, a problem that continues to haunt relations between them to this day. This process of integration of feudatory states continued in parallel with the adoption of a constitution for a parliamentary democracy known as the Republic of India, which came into being in 1950.

India's development journey started in earnest with
the first five-year plan (1951-1956), somewhat based on
the Bombay Plan developed in 1943 but differing in its
approach to implementation. Instead of free markets, Fabian
socialism became the guiding philosophy. State control of
the "commanding heights" of the economy that emphasized
capital-intensive heavy industry, and protectionism in the
pursuit of self-reliance became the norm by 1956. While
agriculture with self-sufficiency in food grains was the focus of
the first five-year plan, heavy industry was sought to be built
during the second five-year plan (1956-61). Reasonable success
was achieved until the border war with China erupted in 1962,
and the second war with Pakistan over Kashmir in 1965 which
eventually derailed the third five-year plan (1961-66) and the
economy.

During the Nehruvian dispensation, India achieved an
average annualized per capita income that ranged between
1% and 1.9%, better than what was obtainable during Raj,
when the British Rule over the Indian subcontinent had merely
produced a per capita income that was less than 1 or even in
the negative.

We may be tempted to dismiss the tangible contributions
the Nehruvian government had made for India to secure
its current place or position among the fast-growing global
economies due to their apparent neglect of grassroots
education, but the regime had bequeathed the nation some
of its top-ranking, globally recognized higher institutions,
including Indian Institutes of Technology (IITS), Indian
Institutes of Management (IIMS), and All India Institutes of
Medical Sciences (AIIMS). However, it is undeniable that many
of the modern-day crop of Indian professionals who later came

on stage to manage the affairs of the nation, between the 18th and 21st centuries, have immensely benefited from at least one of these great institutions of learning.

One area that is not publicly talked about when discussing the Nehruvian model of economy was that the three five-year plans were mathematically drawn up by Prasanta Chandra Mahalanobis, a world-renowned statistician of Indian descent, who put much emphasis on planning rather than its real-life implementations, which turned out to be more difficult than planning itself. Notwithstanding, those plans did not essentially tip India toward becoming a highly industrialized nation right away, but they were instrumental in championing the route or laying the necessary foundations for its subsequent industrialization.

Nehru systemically revamped India's agriculture and caused the sector to become more organized and productive than it was during the Raj. More importantly, according to World Bank data, India's agriculture, in comparison, performed better than that of sub-Saharan Africa; even though Nehru's intention to totally eradicate poverty was not achieved at that time, there was a significant increase in food production up to the year he passed away (1963-1964).

More so, Nehru kickstarted the electrification of India which, as an integral part of industrialization, helped bring about some rapid improvements in local industries that previously relied on human power to drive its operations. He introduced the expansive irrigation campaign designed as a major part of the Nehruvian strategy. According to the World Bank, about 57% of India's arable land has remained drought-prone, hampering agricultural projects that have, even in the

21st century, been identified as the mainstay for the Indian population, employing about 158 million people in 2022.

In hindsight, Nehru deserves to be applauded for his insight in providing funds for regional and state-wide irrigation, a practice that has been maintained or improved upon till today. Whatever the goals Prime Minister Nehru and his team were pursuing, every action they took then was enshrined in socialist ideals that are considered antithesis to market liberalization, the kind that is permissible in a democratic setup.

Despite being referred to as the "Father of Indian Economics", Prime Minister Pamulaparthi Venkata Narasimha Rao was somehow clueless about how to abort the impending 1991 BoP crisis, and the stiff opposition he faced from India's powerful political and social strata that would have wanted to preserve the status quo rendered him quite indecisive. It took the persistent persuasion from his then finance minister, Manmohan Singh to convince him that India was at a risk of facing an economic collapse that could ravage the country if IMF loan terms were not accepted and immediately implemented.

So, as far as India's economic reforms are concerned, Manmohan's handwriting was already all over the wall when he was the finance minister, and it took his ascension to leadership, as a prime minister, to solidify his long-held beliefs that India could no longer do business as usual. Manmohan Singh took confident steps to abolish monopolies and restrictions that were previously imposed on trade practices, a strong and unprecedented course of action that was essential for delicensing industries and promoting rapid development in both public and private sectors.

A critical analysis of Manmohan Singh's policies revealed his preferences when it came to building India's socioeconomic frameworks. As a prominent characteristic in every known democracy, Singh promoted transparent governance by overseeing the passage of the Right to Information Act of 2005, which gave power to all Indian citizens to have unfettered access to public information, instilling in them the much-needed confidence to hold their public officials accountable. He openly demonstrated that he was for governmental flexibility, and this attitude could have motivated Rajya Sabha (India's Upper House Parliament) to pass The Right to Fair Compensation and Transparency in Land Acquisition, Rehabilitation, and Resettlement Act of 2013, which aimed at reforming land acquisition in India by ensuring that families or people whose lands have been taken for whatever purposes could receive equitable compensations in lieu of them.

Nation-building and national security are expected to go hand-in-hand, because it doesn't matter how prosperous a nation is, if it is weak militarily, it may be attacked by an unsuspected enemy. Manmohan Singh oversaw the overhauling of India's internal security through the introduction of a 12-digit, biometric identity card ably managed by the Unique Identification Authority of India. Following the 26/11 terrorist attacks on Mumbai (in 2008), the Manmohan Singh government responded promptly by establishing the National Investigation Agency, supported by the National Investigation Act 2008, which could be invoked anytime to facilitate the investigation and handling of all terrorism-related cases/activities. With other anti-terrorism laws, the Unlawful Activities (Prevention) Act (UPUA) was amended to strengthen India's national security.

On the foreign relations front, Manmohan Singh clearly understood that India needed to foster cooperative, mutually beneficial relationships with other countries such as the United States, China, Japan, Africa, Europe, and those in the Southeast Asian bloc. His closeness to the United States, seen in his readiness to consider signing the India-United States Civil Nuclear Agreement that was publicly maligned by the opposition and even the Left Front parties that had initially supported it, nearly led to the abrupt end of his government. However, his political adversaries could not deny his indefatigable efforts, alongside that of finance minister Palaniappan Chidambaram, which made India to be named the second fastest-growing economy in the world having achieved a growth rate of 9% in 2007.

To adopt a true free-market economy in India by gradually deregulating the market, reducing import tariffs, lowering taxes, and spurring an increase in foreign direct investment, Manmohan Singh also considered the effects such a drastic move could have on the rural economy. To guarantee that every household in the rural communities has income security, he implemented Mahatma Gandhi National Rural Employment Guarantee Act in 2005, which ensured that there was a 100-day employment guarantee for all households in rural areas. Moreover, the National Rural Health Mission (NRHM) his government launched in 2005 aimed at streamlining medical services for people in rural communities. Following the enactment of the 2009 Right to Education Act (RTE) which made education mandatory for children between the ages of 6 and 14, fulfilling article 21A of the Indian Constitution that spells education as the fundamental human right of children, the Manmohan Singh-led government also implemented a 27%

reservation for Other Backward Class (OBC) students in AIIMs, IIMs, and IITs, a decision that was upheld by the Supreme Court of India.

In 2005, Singh's government introduced the Value Added Tax (VAT) as a way of simplifying India's taxation system. He overhauled India's banking system which was previously nationalized and largely unprofitable. He mobilized a widespread cut in government spending and put more funds into infrastructural development that involved building connecting roads and telecommunication.

It is fair to affirm that the Manmohan Singh-led government and that of his predecessor caused a seismic shift in the Indian economy and consequently guided it into the free-market economy that it is today. As their efforts began to yield tangible results, from 1992 to 2005, foreign investment in India increased by 316.9% and the country's GDP expanded from $266 billion in 1991 to $2.3 trillion in 2018. India was able to escape an economic catastrophe that could have shaken it to its foundation had Manmohan Singh not rescued it from the Balance of Payment fiasco when India's foreign debt was estimated to be $72 billion, growing at a rate of 2% while the rupee was reportedly overvalued by 30% and hurting exports.

Good governance isn't a sprint, it is arguably a marathon. India has been able to maintain its economic progress because Prime Minister Modi chose to perpetuate and systematically expand the free-economic policies of his predecessors. We can never assume that every new government would do the same, because a new government may direct India's affairs by adopting different approaches; this is why Indian electorates must painstakingly consider the options they have in the

2024 general elections and discreetly do their part in ensuring that good leaders are provided the continuity they require to complete their transformational works in India.

Chapter 7

Acceleration of India's Journey under Modi: Development and Reforms

What should India's transformation look like? This is a very significant but difficult question because taking India's socialist past and its current "Hindu nationalism" into consideration, it is apparent that India would have to fashion its own, unique, transformational ideals that are enshrined in both democratic and free-economy principles.

India's closest neighbor, China, is a typical example; from Deng Xiaoping to Xi Jinping, Chinese leaders have been quite ambivalent about the kinds of development they would like to see or experience in their country. While staying true to their communist foundation, they equally embraced free-economy practices, in as much as such socioeconomic achievements continue to give their people a better life after pulling almost 800 million Chinese people out of abject poverty, according to the World Bank.

Two recent books have reviewed India's economic progress and prospects. While both are optimistic about the long-run prospects for India, the emphasis is on the need for "deep reforms" or "factor reforms such as land and labor" that require tough political choices for India to realize its full potential. The first book, *India's Long Road* by Vijay Joshi, highlights that even at the current growth rate of 7%, it will not be until 2040 that India's per capita income (at Purchasing Power Parity, PPP) will reach the levels that OECD countries like Portugal enjoy today, which is at the lower end of OECD's per capita income range. The author suggests that India's transformation requires radical economic reforms aimed at "rapid, inclusive, stable, and sustainable growth within a political framework of liberal democracy". These reforms are grouped into seven areas – not mutually exclusive but interconnected: 1) Macroeconomic Stability; 2) Investment Climate; 3) Deep Fiscal Adjustment and a Universal Basic Income; 4) Markets, Ownership, and Regulations; 5) External Economic Engagement; 6) Social Protection and Enablement; and 7) Reform of the State.

The second book, *The Turn of the Tortoise* by T. N. Ninan, suggests three megatrends over the next 10 years. This includes a significant expansion in the scale of Indian markets due to the doubling of India's middle class, the retreat of the state from playing a central role, shifting centers of gravity, and a question mark about the direction of liberal democracy in India. He credits India with sufficient reforms in the product markets, that is, goods and services (with the exception of agriculture) but recognizes that it has not done enough in the factor markets, such as land, labor, capital, and technology/ entrepreneurship. However, the author believes that after Asia's high-growth tiger economies and China, it is now India's turn – therefore, the turn of the tortoise after the hares have run ahead in the race toward prosperity!

Either way, both books concur that India today is at the cusp of achieving greater power status. Its economy is the third largest in PPP terms or fifth in nominal dollar terms (and at the current growth rate, India is poised to become the third largest in nominal terms within the next decade). Not only that, but it also continues to move up in every metric in the Human Development Index (HDI), and its income inequality is about the global average as measured by GINI coefficient. India has started to lead initiatives to combat climate change and loomed large in every aspect of global affairs, raising its voice on important international issues that it used to be previously neutral on.

Even though India is currently classified among the "lower middle-income countries", its HDI and GINI index values are in the middle, and its economy is growing at the fastest rate among all large economies. At 8.6%, India remains the third largest contributor to the global growth rate, ahead of the Eurozone which contributed only 7.9% to the world's growth.

Looking ahead, one can conceptualize what India's transformation will look like – reaching OECD levels of prosperity, human development, and income equality. The questions are: how long will it take, what are the reforms and policies required, and what type of political leadership is capable of taking India to that glorious destination or El Dorado?

Since both of these books review the Modi government's performance during its first two years (2014-2016) only, their perceptions could be judged prematurely. They unanimously lamented the absence of reforms that have since been accomplished, such as the Goods and Services Tax (GST),

Insolvency and Bankruptcy Code (IBC), and Real Estate
Regulations Act (RERA). Even so, the authors acknowledge the
turnaround in macroeconomic stability and the new initiatives
under Modi, yet their accounts do not fully represent the
current state of Indian socioeconomic progress.

Enacted in 2016, the Insolvency and Bankruptcy Code
aims to facilitate the process of resolving failed businesses
and establishing a legal framework for resolving issues of
corporate insolvency between debtors and creditors. IBC came
into effect at the right time as free-market entrepreneurship
became mainstream in India. GST eliminated the complex
taxation structure that was in place before Modi assumed office
and unified India's taxation into a single (national), value-
added regime whereby taxes are collected at the final point
of consumption of goods and services across all the states in
the country. In the same vein, the Real Estate Regulations Act,
promulgated in March 2016, aims to protect homebuyers as
well as boost strategic investments in real estate. To be honest,
RERA provides India's first opportunity to demystify real
estate and open the industry to everyone in the country.

Now that Modi's term is nearly over, it is possible to
measure India's progress under him in objective terms – both
in the absolute or as compared to previous governments. In
this context, it should be noted that all reforms involve change
– too much in too short a time can be counterproductive, the
most recent example of which is the "yellow shirt" agitation
in France in response to Macron's "whirlwind" reform
undertaken within the first two years of his presidency.

For measuring the Modi government's performance, we
use the following metrics: macroeconomic data, global indices,

infrastructure development, political stability, international
stature, social and cultural development, and internal and
external security. In addition, we will review how far reforms
have progressed for each of the categories identified in the
above-mentioned books.

India's GDP growth rate during the Modi era places it
among the fastest-growing economies in the world – as well as
being the fastest-growing "large economy" overtaking China.
The growth rate has also accelerated as compared to the dip in
the last three years under Manmohan Singh, as shown in Table
7.1.

Table 7.1	India's GDP growth rate (%)												
2009-10	2010-11	2011-12	2012-13	2013-14	2014-15	2015-16	2016-17	2017-18	2018-19	2019-20	2020-21	2021-22	2022-23
7.9	8.5	5.2	5.5	6.4	7.4	8.2	7.1	6.7	7.3	4.8	–7.7	8.7	7.2

The GDP growth rate did take a hit during 2016-17, due to
demonetization and GST transition, but has since recovered
and estimated to be around 7.5% during 2017-18. The long-term
benefits of these two reforms are substantial: demonetization
resulted in a more formal economy with growth in the number
of taxpayers, uncovering of fraudulent firms, and increase in
digital payments, while GST established a "common market"
across India by substituting one consolidated tax for several
taxes previously levied by the central and state governments.

Moreover, COVID-19 affected India's growth between 2019
and 2021, as it attained -7.7% during the fiscal year 2020-2021.

However, India returned to amazing growth in 2021-22 when it achieved a growth rate of 8.7% post-COVID-19. This was at a time when many countries were still struggling to deal with different post-COVID-19 headaches.

It is an undeniable fact that all major national transitions often go through short-term pains; whether through implementation challenges or the time needed for the change to be fully accepted, and while it is only natural for opposition to target demonetization and GST, their claims do not hold up to scrutiny. The fiscal deficit has come down from 6.4% in 2013-14 to 3.3%, inflation from double digits to 3-4%, current account deficit is within 1-2%, and the currency has done better than most emerging markets as compared to the strong dollar (even as it has depreciated during the current year).

Overall, the macroeconomic stability has been better than any other regime in independent India. The performance of various governments in the post-reform era is shown in Table 7.2.

Table 7.2   Performance of various governments in the post-reform era

	GDP Growth	Inflation (%)
1991-96	5.1	10.2
1996-98	5.8	8.1
1998-2004	5.9	5.4
2004-09	6.9	5.7
2009-14	6.7	10.1
2014-19	7.3	4.6
2019-23	7.3	9.13

India has made rapid progress under the Modi government,

as acknowledged by various international organizations, and this advancement is remarkable when measured against global economic and social indicators. These are briefly summarized in Table 7.3.

Table 7.3	Advancement of India against global economic and social indicators		
International Index	2014	2018	2022
Ease of doing business (World Bank)	142	77	63
Global Innovation (WIPO)	76	57	40
E-government index (UN)	118	91	105
Travel & Tourism Competitiveness (WEF)	65	40	54
Climate Change performance index	30	14	8
E-participation index (UN)	40	15	105

The development in rural infrastructure and social indicators has been equally impressive.

| Table 7.4 | Development in rural infrastructure and social indicators |

Rural Infrastructure & Social Indicators	2014	2018-2022
Rural road connectivity	55%.	91%
Rural households with electricity	70%	95%
Optical fiber network (to gram panchayats)	0.1%	50%
Rural sanitation coverage	38%	95%
Households with bank accounts	50%	99%
Household with Gas connections	55%	90%
Common Service Centers	84 thousand	300 thousand

Major reforms like the Goods & Services Tax (GST) and Insolvency and Bankruptcy Code (IBC) have been systematically carried out, simplifying India's tax structure and bringing more people and enterprises in the tax net.

| Table 7.5 | India's Tax Structure (2014-2022) |

India's Tax Structure	2014	2018-2022
People filing income tax	38 million	68 million
Enterprises registered for indirect tax	6.6 million	12 million

Perhaps the best way to look at the achievements of any incumbent's term is to ask how the country fared and whether the citizens are better off today versus at the beginning of the term. A recent analysis by Times of India (Feb 2, 2019) is illustrative of the strides made, as well as shortfalls, under the Modi government: India's progress is impressive by any objective criteria: GDP increased in excess of 40%, by $918 billion, and is nearing $3 trillion; per capita income is nearing

$2,000 (twice the level 10 years ago, same as China's in 2006, which is now about $9,000). The government's aspirational goal for the economy is to reach $5 trillion in another five years and $10 trillion in eight years thereafter.

This would be in excess of the most positive scenario visualized in a PricewaterHouseCoopers (PwC) report of 2014. All eligible households now have electricity, 98% of rural households have access to toilets, and 90% of all eligible households have LPG connections and Jan Dhan accounts (this is even more inspirational when you consider that the PwC report projects achieving such metrics by 2034). India's poverty rate, as measured by the Tendulkar method or the World Bank continued its steady decline from 40% to less than 5% estimated currently as shown in Table 7.6.

Table 7.6	India's Poverty Rate Decline– Urban/Rural (%) (est.)			
	2004-05	2011-12	2018	2022
Tendulkar	25.7/41.8	13.7/25.7	NA	9.28/5.27
World Data Lab	NA	9.49/14.05	3.79/4.25	5/0.6

Other important metrics that are worth recognizing are: astonishing improvement in the ease of business rankings from 134 to 77, record Foreign Direct Investment inflows that more than doubled crossing $60 billion in 2017-18, and the reduction in subsidies from its peak of 18.23% of GDP during 2012-13 to 11.96% during 2018-19.

Of course, India continues to lag in terms of its per capita income and Human Development Indices (HDIs) – primarily due to its population and low investment in health and education sectors. The Modi government understands these challenges and has undertaken groundbreaking healthcare and education reforms. Its recently launched Ayushman Bharat Scheme is the world's largest – not a surprise given India's population but audacious in scope and difficult to implement.

Overall India continues to lag behind China by about 10 to 15 years in its economic and social progress depending upon whichever metric you choose. This is not surprising since India's economic reforms came 13 years later, in 1991 versus 1978. Indeed, the surprise is that India has been able to keep pace in the race. The Modi government has certainly reduced the gap and laid the appropriate foundation for India's imminent, countrywide transformation – but the truth is that much more remains to be done to achieve this!

Chapter 8

Building on the Foundation: Reforms and Development Needed for India's Transformation

In this chapter, we will review what India's realistic transformation should look like with regard to the growth trajectory needed to achieve the vision and the strategies and reforms that are critical as next steps.

Given India's size, military might and strategic weight or influence in international affairs will naturally follow once it becomes the third largest economy. From all indications, and considering its current giant socioeconomic leaps, it is clear that nothing can stop India from becoming the world's third-largest economy and the third superpower alongside the United States and China.

Currently, India is classified as an upper-middle-income country with a per capita GDP of about $2,000 (nominal) or $8,000 (PPP) and an HDI of 0.64. For comparison, the current average Global per capita GDP is about $12,000 (nominal) or $18,000 (PPP) – the same as that of China today. The gap is even more relative to the developed economies of the OECD countries which have an average per capita GDP of about $42,500 – approximately three times the global average.

The bottom line is that India has a mountain to climb when it comes to ensuring the prosperity of its citizens. This entails that it needs to double its current per capita GDP at PPP to reach the global average and do so more than five times to reach the level of developed economies today.

Another relevant comparison is India's per capita GDP at PPP trend versus China's and the United States' since these three are expected to emerge as the world's largest economies by 2030. Even as late as 1991, when India began to dismantle its "Licence-Permit Raj", its per capita GDP at the PPP rate was ahead of China's ($1169 versus $983 in 1990). However, the situation had changed by 1995 when China had pulled ahead and the gap has continued to increase in the quarter century since then.

While India's progress is commendable, with a fivefold increase over three decades, China has raced ahead with a tenfold economic expansion during the same period. The average Indian is now one-eighth as prosperous as the average American as compared to one-twentieth a generation ago – however a major gap has opened up relative to China even though the starting point was comparable, and this remains a matter of serious concern.

Whether India could have done any better with its democratic setup and coalition governments is arguable – some economists hold the view that India pays a "democracy premium" of as much as a 2% reduction in its growth rate, while others posit that deeper reforms were needed which are difficult to implement in a "soft state" like India. Either way, the capacity of the Indian state to deliver has been far short of China, and India's leadership needs to seriously examine what crucial steps are needed to step up the growth rate. Some obvious steps include investing in education and healthcare to take advantage of the demographic dividend, building institutional capability through merit-based recruitment and promotions, and re-engineering governmental processes.

Table 8.1 shows the trends in per capita GDP in PPP dollars for India, China, and the United States from 1995 onwards, both in absolute as well as in indexed terms.

Table 8.1	India's per capita income as compared to China and the United States [PPP $ (Index)]						
	1995	**2000**	**2005**	**2010**	**2015**	**2018**	**2022**
India	1529	2026	2903	4425	6255	7784	7333
	(5)	(6)	(7)	(9)	(11)	(12)	
China	1870	2930	5064	9252	14330	18120	21476
	(6)	(8)	(11)	(19)	(25)	(29)	
US	28671	36433	48310	56437	62527	65067	65423
	(100)	(100)	(100)	(100)	(100)	(100)	

Arguably, the Human Development Index (HDI) is a more important metric for measuring significant progress recorded by any nation, even though it is not as widely used as GDP because it is more difficult to calculate and understand. It incorporates life expectancy, education, asset ownership, and income inequality in addition to income, to measure development across countries which are grouped into four categories: very high, high, medium, and low with corresponding HDI ranges of more than 0.80, between 0.7 and

0.8, 0.55 to 0.7, and 0.35 to 0.55. China has recently moved up to a high HDI of 0.752, while India is a medium HDI country at 0.64.

We judge India's transformation as reaching per capita income at purchasing power parity four times its current value (which translates into about a third of the United States'), along with the HDI exceeding 0.80 – which would put India in the range of OECD countries – and slightly ahead of China today. However, China is still expected to be further ahead by then as it will also continue to grow its economy, albeit at slower growth rates in the next decade.

While such an aspiration for India may appear to be unrealistic, it is what China has been able to do during the past generation with a GDP growth rate of 9%. India has not been too far below China with a growth rate of around 7%. If India could achieve a 9% rate of GDP growth compared to the 7.3% average growth rate during the past five years, the desired per capita income could be achieved in 15 to 25 years (even after assuming population growth at the current rates of 0.7% annually, which is likely to decline even further).

Predicting the trajectory of HDI is far more difficult since each country in the index is also moving forward at the same time, albeit at different rates, but going by the past trends an incremental 0.16 should be achievable at about the same time.

The strategic implications of such a projected transformation for India are enormous: once it is clearly ranked the third-largest economy in both nominal and purchasing power parity terms, it would be difficult to deny its entry into the Security Council at the United Nations, and India's relative strengths vis-à-vis its constant threats – China and Pakistan – will significantly increase.

China's growth rate has slipped behind India's in recent years, while Pakistan's has been consistently behind since India's reforms in 1991. IMF data shows India's overall GDP now being only nine years behind China's – which could further reduce to five years at the projected future growth rates. Both China and India are major trading partners, and multinationals from both countries invest in each other. As for defense, India has geography on its side as it is separated by the Himalayas and the oceans, its nuclear capability is sufficient to thwart China, and strategic alliances are in place to defend its interests in the Indo-Pacific region.

Some recent events have indicated that India is not taking its security lightly and, despite being a trade partner with China, it still considers it as a formidable, potential threat similar to Pakistan. For instance, India stood its ground in the Doklam confrontation with China in 2017, which is often referred to as the China-India border standoff. No doubt, Chinese leadership learned an important lesson about India's doggedness during the standoff and has since chosen to have a much deeper diplomatic engagement with India. The likely future scenario is that of cooperation in trade and competition for strategic parity – similar to the relationship between China and the United States.

As for Pakistan, it has steadily lost ground to India in the race for prosperity; its per capita income has gone from being one-third more to one-third less as compared to India in the course of the last two decades. It should be noted that there was a time when the average Pakistani was substantially better off than an Indian. However, the policies pursued plus the higher population growth rate have contributed to a steady decline in Pakistan's relative position as compared to India – and there is no sign of this trend changing any time soon.

Therefore, if India were to achieve the transformation envisaged, it could substantially reduce the threat of China's dominance – especially as the alliance between the "Quad" countries (India, Japan, Australia, and the US) evolves – as well as render its alliance with Pakistan meaningless. The total and per capita GDP trends for India and Pakistan are shown in Table 8.2.

Table 8.2	Total GDP and per capita GDP for India and Pakistan (in billions)					
	2000	2005	2010	2015	2018	2022
India-Nominal GDP (Billion $)	476	834	1708	2089	2848	3530
India-per capita GDP (PPP $)	2026	2616	4425	6625	7784	7096
Pakistan-Nominal GDP (Billion $)	80	118	177	271	307	375
Pakistan-per capita (PPP $)	2700	3503	4133	4908	5677	5451

Source: IMF

At current projections by the IMF, the gap between the economies of India and Pakistan and the prosperity of their populations will continue to increase in the foreseeable future. Indeed, India's economy will be 10 times bigger than Pakistan's, with annual growth equal to that of Pakistan's entire economy within the decade. Such a differential will make it impossible for Pakistan to compete with India in any sphere –

even though it can carry out its asymmetric war with India due to its nuclear parity, albeit at great cost to the prosperity of its citizens.

Table 8.3	Projected nominal GDP and per capita GDP at PPP– India & Pakistan (2019-23)				
	2019	**2020**	**2021**	**2022**	**2023**
India–Nominal GDP (Billion $)	3155	3477	3832	4226	4663
India–Per Capita GDP (PPP $)	8461	9189	9989	10846	11637
Pakistan–Nominal GDP (Billion $)	342	371	406	449	501
Pakistan–Per Capita GDP (PPP $)	5959	6254	6066	6881	7213

Source: IMF

The key issue then is that of raising the trajectory of India's development – such that its transformation occurs sooner than later, say in 15 years, versus 20 to 25 years. Niti Aayog, the government's think tank and primary development agency, has recently suggested that an incremental 1% GDP growth can be achieved through further reforms. International organizations like the IMF and World Bank, as well as rating agencies like S&P and Moody's forecast India's near-term growth accelerating from 7.5 to 8%. So, the obvious questions are: what are these reforms, and whether they can be done within India's democratic, social, and cultural setup?

We, along with many other economists and political commentators, have characterized the reforms carried out so far in India to be "partial"– while "License & Permit Raj" has been abolished, protectionist policies abandoned, and the economy opened up as well as integrated within the global economy, much remains to be done. We list the following reforms that are still required, and if systematically carried out, can be instrumental in India's quick transformation:

- **Land and Labor reforms – making it easier to acquire land and utilize labor agriculture reforms that would guarantee unrestricted trade and direct cash transfer instead of subsidies**

  In their current forms, India's land reforms are inadequate because they do not summarily address the existing problems of the zamindari system, inability to consolidate land holdings, lack of necessary records digitalization, and revolving tenancy.

  India needs to take up land reforms now or it may lose another golden decade to bring the much-needed prosperity to its people. It is believed that well-coordinated reforms would make land available to those who need it for large-scale farming. This will not only increase productivity in the already segmented agrarian sector, but it will also pull millions of Indian households that absolutely depend on agriculture for their survival out of abject poverty.

  In the same way, to sustain the already gained economic momentum in India, it should undertake further liberalization of its labor system. If we are going to become a magnet for foreign investors, we cannot continue to push back our labor reforms. India should put in place modalities that will guarantee a universal minimum wage for all workers in its states and unions; it must ensure that workers are paid on time, and their health and working conditions are taken into account. Indian workers deserve a well-planned social security system that will make sure that they have pensions and other post-retirement financial incentives to fall back on when they can no longer work. As it is now in India, opening our doors to foreign companies and investors without the appropriate labor reforms in place will only allow bad foreign companies to take advantage of hardworking Indian workers, and they will be worse off when cheated by their foreign employers.

- **Retail sector – opening up a multi-brand retail supply chain that would make it easy for manufacturers and/or producers of all goods/services to market their products without any hassles, and for consumers to have unfettered access to their desired products**

Regarded as the 5th largest retail distribution channel, India has come of age in its downstream retailing business which, in 2022, brought in a whopping $836 billion. Interestingly enough, 81.5% of that amount was contributed by Indian traditional retail.

Since COVID-19 has caused a shift in India's retail sector and encouraged online shopping, this dramatic change has led to a significant increase in the number of e-commerce stores in India, with some international brands such as Amazon, Alibaba, and eBay coming into India, operating alongside the local e-commerce companies like Flipkart, Myntra, IndiaMart, etc. India's retail industry is poised for massive growth as the deep-pocketed, Indian middle-class and the adventurous Gen Z are exposed to international brands (goods/services).

- **Judicial reforms – need for speed, improving selection process, and increasing tenure for the judiciary**

  In addition to providing the judges and magistrates with good working and living conditions, it is equally important to set a mandatory retirement age for them to ensure that only capable judges are left on the benches.

  Currently, India adopts the common law system; however, this can be reformed by rightly codifying the laws for easier reference. It may also be necessary to replace the existing inquisitorial system with an adversarial system. Above all, the judiciary must be granted independence as far as prosecuting cases are concerned; India will be better for it if the judiciary is not unduly manipulated by politics.

- **Further opening of the economy – no restriction on investment/FDI in any sector and abolition of currency controls**

  It is an optimistic expectation that India will someday liberalize all its sectors and allow more inflow of foreign direct investments. On records, India's FDIs have grown enormously between April 2000 and March 2023, valued at $919 bn. Interestingly enough, $595.25 bn of that flocked to the country within the last nine years, under Prime Minister Modi. The top five sectors getting the largest share of the FDIs during 2022-2023 are the Service Sector (Financial, Banking, Insurance, Non-Fin/ Business,

Outsourcing, R&D, Courier, Tech. Testing and Analysis, Other) (16%), Computer Software & Hardware (15%), Trading (6%), Telecommunications (6%) and Automobile Industry (5%) respectively.

While some of the sectors are now 100% automatically permitted for FDIs, others such as digital/print media, health, multi-brand retail trading, pharmaceuticals, defense, broadcasting content services, etc. still require some levels of governmental approvals before foreign investors could set up those industries. Foreign investors are not allowed at all to go into the prohibited sectors, such as establishing lottery businesses, gambling, and betting, real estate business of constructing farmhouses, manufacturing cigars and tobaccos, railway operations, and so on.

- **Health and Education reforms – improving healthcare and providing free school/skill acquisition education**

The Indian health sector has come a long way as the Modi government increased the annual budget for healthcare services and launched some revolutionizing healthcare services. However, more reforms are still required for everyone to have access to high-quality healthcare. Some of the expected reforms include facilitating the partnership between the public and private healthcare providers, most especially in the urban areas to guarantee that people can receive medical attention when needed and avoid hospital congestion. India also should ensure that a comprehensive health insurance policy is initiated so that people can enjoy affordable healthcare services and avoid expensive, out-of-pocket payments for their medical services. It is also necessary that the rural health system be expanded so that more hospitals and clinics can be set up to accommodate everyone who urgently needs medical treatment.

- **Defense – achieve import/export net self-sufficiency and balance between different branches (as is being done by China) of defense forces**

Reforming India has seemed like the most difficult task any Indian prime minister will ever try to take on, judging by the way it has been strongly opposed by both the bureaucracy and the military officers themselves. Many perceived transforming the military, which has remained rooted in 19402 and 19502 practices, would weaken the Indian military. On the other hand, the military officers thought their relevance would be challenged if their statutory functions were eliminated or streamlined. These discordant voices against reforming the Indian forces make running the affairs of the military quite expensive, and the heightened concern that they are not well-prepared for modern warfare tore many politicians apart, with some pushing for the Indian military's reform while others stood against it.

When he came to power in 2014, Prime Minister Modi faced the same complex issue, but instead of balking at it, he went straight ahead to implement some of the recommendations past military and civil leaders had made about the best approaches for reforming the Indian military. This included establishing the office of a Chief Defense (CDS) Staff, who will be overseeing everything relating to the defense of the country – its territories, internal security, and cybersecurity.

Based on the recommendations, the Modi government created three new joint functional commands: the Defence Space Agency, the Armed Forces Special Operations Division, and the Defence Cyber Agency. True to his promise, Modi, in December 2019, announced General Bipin Rawat as the new India's Chief of Defence Staff, tasked with managing all issues concerning India's Armed Forces.

We think there are still other defense reforms that should be carried out for our Armed Forces to be as capable as other superpowers. The more prosperous a nation becomes, the more imperative it is to defend its citizens and wealth. Over the years, China has invested heavily in its defense, primarily to ward off any potential attacks from the US or other superpowers. There are no indications that China would be willing to start a war with its current allies, but no one can foresee any preemptive attacks that might be aimed at challenging China's increasing economic dominance.

- **Climate change and environment – meeting or exceeding Paris COP 21 commitments by reducing emissions and reducing usage of fossil fuels**

Following its active participation in COP 21, India is proposing new, environment-friendly approaches to living. In addition to transitioning from coal-based to renewable energy, the country is also seriously looking at establishing smart, environmentally green cities where the buildings and amenities will be powered naturally. Such projects have already been started, which include the 100 Smart Cities Project and the National Solar Mission.

India cannot afford to be exposed to the debilitating impacts of climate change, which may include extreme heat, reduction in groundwater level, drought, health issues, food security and energy, security problems, etc. Never seeming to be short of ideas to revamp every aspect of India's socioeconomy, Prime Minister Modi came up with five programs to initiate Green India, following the country's drop from 141 in 2014 to 177 in 2018 on the Global Environmental Performance Index. These programs include:

1. **Namani Gange Programme** – aims at conserving and preserving the Gange River

2. **Green Skill Development Programme** – set up to pass green skills to young people

3. **Swachh Bharat Abhiyan** – a national cleanliness drive making sure every place in cities, towns, and villages is routinely cleaned

4. **Toilets before Temples** – The government vowed to build several household toilets and encourage people to use them before erecting new temples. This promise reduced the instances of open defecation.

5. **Compensatory Afforestation Fund Act (CAMPA)** – makes it mandatory for a person or a business that wants to cut trees or forests and use them for non-forest purposes to be charged for that action taken

The recent book *India's Long Road: The Search for Prosperity* by Vijay Joshi has put forward the need for radical reforms in detail without which any transformation is unlikely. We discuss these reforms briefly and the possibility of accomplishing these under various leadership assumptions.

Land and labor continue to be a burdensome barrier for any infrastructure or industrial project in democratic India, in sharp contrast to communist China. The "eminent domain" rights of the state that prevailed earlier were replaced by the UPA government whereby not only is compensation to be given which is several times the market value but also social sanctions have been imposed that lengthen the timeline considerably. The BJP government tried to reform the land acquisition process but was stymied by the opposition. It should be noted that the same BJP party had not opposed this very policy when it was in the opposition – such indeed is the reality of India, whether or not it can be said for all democracies.

Similarly, the existing labor laws make it difficult to hire or fire employees, and the weak labor regulations enable enterprises to prefer hiring poorly paid contract workers. The net result is that the private enterprise shies away from labor-intensive production. Even now countries like Vietnam and Bangladesh have marched ahead of India in labor-intensive industries, such as garments, of which production is being moved out of China due to increasing costs there. The Modi government has left labor reforms to the states, realizing the futility of being able to enact the legislation necessary, lacking a majority in the Upper House.

India's overall agricultural productivity is less than half of China's. In 2023, India produced 235 million tons of food grains from 135 million hectares of arable land (the second highest in the world) as compared to China's 100 million hectares (Source: PwC report on India, Achieving the winning leap, 2014). India's current production of 285 million tons could easily be increased with better inputs, post-harvest storage and streamlined transport facilities or networks, and open markets that empower farmers to freely choose where to sell their produce.

However, while the Modi government has undertaken some reforms and better inputs through soil health cards, better pricing through minimum support pricing at 150% of cost covering more crops, supply chain improvements, and value addition through food processing, it has not been enough to alleviate farm distress. Further market reforms and unrestricted exports are needed to tap India's agriculture potential.

India has been slow in opening its retail sector as compared to China. Even now political considerations have come in the way of opening up multi-brand retail to foreign companies. The fear is that it would affect small "mom and pop" retailers who are one of the key segments of the electorate that supports the ruling dispensation. This has resulted in organized retail still being less than 15% of the total retail sector, far behind China, Korea, and other ASEAN countries. This has prevented the buildup of economies of scale that eventually benefit the consumer, slow development of the supply chains and technological deployment, and higher quality of retail jobs. While there can be no doubt that multi-brand retail will be opened up eventually, the sooner the better.

While India's judicial process is criticized on many fronts – from the slow speed of legal proceedings to judicial appointments – attempts to reform it have been incremental. While people's courts (Lok Adalats) have been set up and efforts made to reform the appointments to the higher echelons of the judiciary, there is a need to review the entire system. The short tenure of the Chief Justice of the Supreme Court, the retirement age of the justices, the need for a national judicial service, and increasing the number of judges are all, long-pending issues. Tackling these issues is likely going to require constitutional amendments which most political leaders are loath to touch lest they be accused of interfering with the independence of the judiciary.

India has come a long way from the dark days when Indians could only get taxi fare ($32 or $16) when traveling to another country, or when the License/Permit Raj erected such barriers to foreign investment that most multinational companies either stayed away or assigned the lowest priority to India. Today, Indians can exchange currencies easily and foreign investors are welcome. Foreign investments come through the automatic approval route with some exceptions.

However, as compared to China or other developed economies, India is still more restrictive with respect to capital account inflows and majority ownership of companies. With India being the fifth largest economy at market exchange rates, and third largest by purchasing power parity, the need for any such restrictions must be reviewed.

Resource constraints have resulted in India's under-investment in health and education over the years. The Modi government has recognized this and given priority to health through its Ayushman Bharat health insurance scheme for the poor, opening new higher education institutions and giving more autonomy to selected institutions. Skill India program is aimed at vocational training. Considering all the great steps taken in the direction so far by the Modi administration, India is still in a catch-up mode and more emphasis on investment will be required just to achieve parity with its peers among emerging economies, let alone developed countries.

India has been the world's largest importer of defense equipment in recent years. While the Modi government has recognized this deficiency and tried to build indigenous, military capabilities, progress has been slow. Building such capabilities takes time and foreign investment in the defense sector has been low due to restrictions on majority control of defense enterprises. Political opposition also continues to stall advancement in this defense sector. India needs to seriously examine whether the incremental reforms in this sector are likely to meet the ambitious goals articulated by its leaders and focus on attracting multinational investment in defense industries – that's where much of the technology is, and it is in India's strategic interest to somehow enable its transfer, it's as simple as that – but much easier said than done!

Climate change and other environmental hazards pose the greatest danger to the future of India, as well as China, due to the sheer size of their populations. The resource requirements for raising their populations to the same level of prosperity as the developed countries are enormous, and the impact of their economic progress is already straining their environment. The pollution levels in both countries are already the highest in the world. Water availability, falling water tables, and desertification are major challenges in both countries. Just as Japan stalled due to demographic factors, climate change, and environmental problems can be a "showstopper" in the Indian story. Fortunately, the Indian government is alive to this threat and is taking cautious steps to mitigate this threat. Continued focus and accelerated implementation of renewable energy policies, production of electric cars, reduction in the use of water through drip irrigation, increasing the proportion of forests and green cover in land use, continued reduction in fossil fuel consumption, etc. are some of the strategic measures that can be taken.

As a matter of fact, the challenges on India's path are enormous, and it cannot be summarily assumed that India can continue to progress on its current trajectory. Indeed countries inevitably slow down when confronted with mountainous challenges such as those mentioned above, and the PwC report on India's winning leap had already factored in such a slowdown. India's growth rate needs to be accelerated, which in turn requires further reforms – and such development must not come at the expense of the environment. What happens next depends very much on the wisdom of the electorate exercising their electoral rights to keep a transformational leader in power to better their lives and that of the future generations.

Modi's reforms and consistent campaign against corruption have aroused much hostility towards him, which is not unexpected. Moreover, his disruption of dynastic politics has caused the opposition to come together to prevent another term for him. Whatever the outcome of the forthcoming elections, we hope that the need for these reforms will not be forgotten in the din of politics.

This page is intentionally left blank

Chapter 9

Characteristics of A Transformational Leader and Why India Needs One?

In this chapter, we review the characteristics of transformational leaders and why India requires one at the current stage of its development. The characteristics are derived from our analysis of the historical records of transformational leaders; every leader has these qualities to some degree, as well as weaknesses – their successes largely depended both on the situations or challenges they faced and the degree to which their personalities demonstrated the much-needed characteristics.

The reason India needs a transformational leader is to carry out the deep reforms required, especially in land and labor, and to further step up its growth rate beyond what has been possible so far, which is often rationalized as the discount due to its democratic, political system, as compared to China, Taiwan, or South Korea.

The characteristics of transformational leaders are listed below, with further discussion and specific examples thereafter. These characteristics are like ingredients in a recipe – and different leaders have different recipes for success. However, all of them possess the following characteristics to some degree:

- **Impeccable Integrity (honest, incorruptible, principle-driven):** Leaders who have track records of being corrupt and dishonest will have a hard time convincing their followers to play fair. More often than not, followers imitate their leaders' actions and styles of governance. No one is perfect, but if you are going to lead a group of people, you – the leader – must be above board. In life, character is the main currency we pay for acceptance. If a leader is notorious for being deceptive and unreliable on most occasions, it is almost impossible for such a leader to convince people to support him in whatever cause he may be promoting.

- **Worldwide Credibility (charismatic with track records of achievement):** In the 21st century, any leader who is inward-looking and shunning international partnerships will plunge his citizens far into obscurity and shut them out of possible, cross-border opportunities in an age where a small-scale trader in any Indian village can get online and sell his/her merchandise to international customers several thousands of kilometers on e-commerce platforms.

  Prime Minister Modi has been called different nicknames – he is a showman, they would say. To be honest, there is nothing if a leader chooses to display his achievements for the whole world to see, as long as his hands are clean and his actions are helpful to his goal of transforming his beloved country.

- **Great (Communicator) Connectivity (oratorical and great communication skills):** Some people allege that the Manmohan Singh dispensation had a communication problem because they failed to carry the citizenry along while attempting to lay the foundations that the Prime Minister was building on and expanding at an alarming rate now. They could be right, to a certain extent, because leaders who cannot talk to the people they govern may lose them over time. There is nothing as risky as allowing a vacuum to exist between leaders and their followers, and due to this problem of incommunicado, the opposition will get the chance to pounce on the confused populace and stir troubling misinformation.

The former US President, Barack Obama, was able to draw people to him due to his oratorical skill, long before he had the hope of winning the US presidency. A leader like Mahatma Gandhi did not need to use any weapons to fight the colonizers; his voice and personal conviction were all the tools he used to his constant advantage to rally people around him.

- **Powerful Visionary (big picture thinker who can see the "total system.")**: Visionary leaders can picture the destination in their minds before taking their people on a transformational journey. Lee Kuan Yew was fond of saying that he wanted Singapore to be self-reliant, an inclusive nation-state, and a place where integrity reigns. While pursuing socioeconomic revitalization for his people, he never seemed to take his eyes off his initial visions for Singapore.

A visionary, in reality, sees opportunities where others perceive impossibilities. He will never shy away from dreaming big and using all his skills, experiences, and influence to pursue his dreams. It is not that they don't see an obstacle blocking their way of progress, but instead of getting cowered by it, they will choose to use the obstacle as a step up the ladder of success.

- **Strategic Thinker (defining and selecting actions to achieve the vision):** Having a clueless leader in power is more dangerous than having no leader at all. Leadership is a difficult task, and it is quite demanding. When leaders face some complicated challenges, they will have to solely rely on their intelligence to quickly come up with the most suitable solutions. The ability to think strategically and skillfully move the pieces, like in a chess game, to find a lasting solution to a problem differentiates strategic thinkers from confused ones.

- **Demanding Executionary (implementation ability, managing process, and events):** A common pitfall on the path of transformational leaders is finding themselves hamstrung by unforeseen forces or challenges, which may include opposition preventing legislation from being passed or their citizens protesting against their unpopular policies. However, a shrewd, pragmatic leader would find a way to maneuver the circumstances to his favor and get things done, even if it may happen at a slower rate. As they say, for a proactive leader, it is better late than never!

- **Practical and Pragmatic (understanding constraints and choosing what is possible):** Setting unrealistic expectations or projects is one of the reasons national policies fail. Conscientious leaders must understand their limitations and restrictions based on the available resources before formulating policies that may be beyond their power to actualize. It takes fearless pragmatism for a leader to decide to change or transform the status quo. In most nations, people like to do the most convenient thing, just like the past Indian leaders had, causing their critics to assume that their slowness in reforming the country has something to do with Hinduism's slow rate.

- **Resolute and Resilient (staying the course, bouncing back despite defeats):** Governance isn't always a smooth-sailing affair – there are definitely going to be bumps and hindrances along the way. At this junction, the leader at the helm must demonstrate a great deal of resiliency or resoluteness. Nothing gets done by just making an elaborate plan on paper – the fieldwork, in this case, the actual leadership will be intentionally or unintentionally misunderstood, challenged, and repressed.

- **Continuous Learner (accepting new ideas, able to think out of the box):** The evolving aspect of any leader is quite essential; in this modern dispensation, things change quickly, and it won't take a long time for an old-styled, inward-looking technocrat to discover that his leadership style can't perfectly handle some modern challenges. A great leader stays ahead of others by constantly learning and adjusting his methodologies or approaches.

- **Tireless Energy (work ethics, driven to achieve their vision):** No one assumes leading a nation or even a local organization would be easy. It is one of the most difficult jobs in the world, and it takes time, energy, dedication, and all the physical strength a leader can muster. This is why a proactive leader must exude boundless energy and optimism. The most important aspect of leadership is that people somehow follow in the footsteps of their leaders. If they are lukewarm and unimpressive, we could expect their followers to exhibit the same traits. However, down-to-earth leaders always motivate their followers to perform their best, because they would be held accountable for their performances.

Transformational leaders always have impeccable integrity– in the manner of *"Caesar's wife who must be beyond suspicion"*– to attract mass followers, even to the point of "cult followership".

Belief in their integrity is the foundation on which their credibility rests and may be considered the necessary (but not sufficient) condition to become a transformational leader. Integrity in this context is not limited to financial integrity, it encompasses intellectual and moral integrity as well. Such leaders stick to their ideology even as they learn and refine it through experience, and their actions reflect their firm beliefs. They can seldom be accused of being a hypocrite, by either their followers or opponents, but they always seek to do the right thing in their actions.

Credibility, of course, is the "coin of the realm"– nothing works without it. One cannot be a leader, let alone a transformational leader, without it. Followers' belief in the credibility of their leaders is essential to ensure that they continue to follow and take direction from their leaders. Transformational leaders are invariably role models for their followers through their thoughts and actions. Maintaining credibility is essential for leaders – it not only immunizes them from attacks from their opposition but ensures that their base is intact. And once credibility is lost, it is seldom regained – just as shattered glass cannot be put together again! It is also important to note that in this globally connected world, it is not enough to have credibility within one's own realm as transformation inevitably requires support and interaction with other international powers.

Connectivity requires oratory skills, listening skills, personal relationship-building, and the ability to interact with masses – including kissing babies, hugging mothers, and shaking hands. It can include showmanship to a certain degree, as well as an ability to communicate their ideas in simple, quotable terms – such as Deng Xiaoping's overturning communist orthodoxy on its head by stating that *"it does not matter whether a cat is white or black as long as it catches mice"*. They also understand the importance of publicizing – and that one must communicate the message over and over to make sure it registers with the masses; there is no such thing as over-communication! Obviously, connectivity alone does not make for a transformational leader. Hitler mesmerized the masses but left Germany in ruins because he did not have many of the other characteristics needed to succeed.

Without a doubt, all leaders have a vision; however, not all are purpose-driven or can create a powerful enough vision to change the status quo. Transformational leaders are always "big picture thinkers" who see the "total system", interrelationships between its components, and where strategic leverage can be had to move towards their visions. They are good at three things: creating dissatisfaction with the status quo, articulating their vision, and identifying the practical steps their followers can take to achieve their vision. As an example, Mahatma Gandhi created dissatisfaction with the status quo through his opposition to the salt tax and imported clothing, articulated his vision for an independent and socially transformed India, and showed that peaceful resistance in which the masses could easily participate (instead of risking their lives in violence) was the most practical path to success.

Success in any complex task requires strategies and tactics – and national transformation is indeed the most complex of all tasks. There are many paths to take and success requires making the correct strategic choices and actions needed to implement the strategy. Transformational leaders can select the right strategy and follow up with the tactical actions required – even if it is done through trial and error with course correction when needed.

Comparing the strategic choices and tactics of Deng Xiaoping during the post-Mao era with that of India's leaders and one gets the point – it took 13 years and a BoP crisis for India to change course after China, and even then only through partial reforms. How one wishes that the correct choice between capitalism and socialism, or between neutrality versus proactive alliances in the national interest, had been made by India's leaders after independence. Arguably, India could have been much further ahead on its road to national transformation instead of having lost a generation and trailing China by far today – even though both nations were shoulder-to-shoulder at the beginning of the race.

Transformational leaders are always demanding, set extensive goals and see their plans through successful implementation– and not just getting started. They are masters at managing processes and events, monitoring progress, identifying and overcoming barriers, and carrying on until their vision is fully realized. They do not just lay foundation stones and then disappear, as has unfortunately been the case with many of the leaders in emerging countries, including India, but ensure the absolute execution of their strategies.

We call such leaders "Executionaries" to emphasize the point that the less glamorous task of execution is as important as the vision or the strategy.

In the Indian context, Modi's execution skills stand out to any objective observer, even though the opposition and, sometimes, some within his own party have patronizingly referred to him as an "event manager" fond of executing projects.

Achieving success requires being pragmatic and not dogmatic – an essential quality for taking the majority along. This involves not sacrificing the possible in search for the ideal and making course corrections when and where appropriate. Without pragmatism, leaders run the risk of getting too far ahead of followers or increasing the resistance of opponents. Incrementalism versus radicalism can often be the difference between success and failure. It can enable the leader to stay in power long enough to achieve their vision. History is witness to many failures of idealists who refused to be practical or pragmatic – they either built "castles in the air" or lost power, sometimes even their head (hence the saying that every revolution eats its children), ending up as well-meaning failures.

The most recent example of this is Macron's recent debacle in France – attributed by many observers as being due to his "reform blitz" post-election and arrogance in not being practical or pragmatic enough to understand the limits of his mandate.

Resoluteness and resilience are critical characteristics – since every transformation requires tough decisions, obstacles and resistance, failure at times, and staying the course even if repeated efforts are needed in pursuit of the leaders' goals. The ability to "bounce back" even after a significant personal, or electoral loss, or after incarceration or even exile, is typical of every transformational leader.

Lincoln's carrying on after the loss of his son, Roosevelt's rise even after his disability due to polio, Churchill's years in political isolation, Hitler's imprisonment before coming to power, Mao's long march, Indira Gandhi's coming back to power, Deng Xiaoping after Tiananmen Square events, Modi after Godhra riots, etc. are examples of leaders' resoluteness or resilience – even though not all those leaders' cited were transformational.

An open mind to new ideas or technologies and constant learning is another hallmark of transformational leaders. While their intellectual integrity may cause them to stick to their convictions or ideology, they adapt in pursuit of their vision. They learn from their mistakes and understand that not everything works out but it is important to be decisive and action-oriented. They are willing to take risks and are not afraid of innovation, indeed they encourage it as long as it does not get in the way.

In the course of India's journey, many leaders opposed the introduction of new technologies or opposed the teaching of English without understanding their impact on the productivity or competitiveness of Indians. Fortunately, leaders like Rajiv Gandhi and Narendra Modi stand out as major exceptions and deserve credit for the introduction of new technologies in governance.

Nothing is possible in life without energy – and so it is when it comes to leadership. Transformational leaders are passionate and single-minded in the pursuit of their vision. They never seem to feel tired; indeed, they seem to derive energy from their actions and act as role models for their followers. Their tireless energy is an integral part of their credibility. They are never seen as "reluctant politicians" or "itinerant leaders", instead they are admired by their followers for their energy – even if often derided as driven, obsessed, or possessed by their opponents, and their actions construed as "grandstanding or optics". Their energy can be greatly influential in changing the behavior of other leaders – to those who choose to follow them or to their competitors to stay in the game. Their energy inspires the masses and enhances their credibility. The most obvious example in India's polity is Modi's energy – whether it be in pursuit of electoral success, development projects, or enhancing India's stature abroad, he truly embodies a powerful, infectious energy.

All leaders have opponents and enemies – it is par for the course! Transformational leaders always make fierce enemies because of their decisiveness and tough decisions. And while we have chosen not to make it a characteristic, this point should be noted as well. Arguably the ability to overcome enemies can be a characteristic or it can be considered to be a part of being resolute. In any case, such leaders do not fear enemies when pursuing their vision or goals. After all Lincoln, Gandhi, and Park Chung Hee were assassinated; Roosevelt, Churchill, Deng Xiaoping, Lee Kuan Yew had fierce enemies, and so on. Roosevelt is famously quoted as having said *"judge me by the enemies I make"*. Indeed the task of transformation is such that it is inevitable to arouse opposition and create fierce enemies; however, no transformational leader is deterred by the possibility of such an outcome!

With India having progressed steadily since 1991, the obvious question is – why is a transformational leader needed? First and foremost is the opportunity: India is on the cusp of becoming a global power, it is already the third-largest economy at purchasing power parity and fifth-largest at market exchange rates. India is projected to become the third-largest economy by both metrics – and the second-largest after China by 2050 (Price Waterhouse Cooper's reports: The world in 2050).

However, there is no guarantee that this will happen – GDP growth inevitably slows down as economies mature, as has happened in China recently: it is a natural outcome of achieving more and more of the potential, and larger base effect that requires expanding the incremental growth every year to achieve the same percentage growth.

Still, there is a need to grow even faster – in terms of nominal per capita GDP, India ranks 142nd in the world – and while there has been impressive progress in poverty reduction, the absolute number of the poor remains the highest in the world (though the latest figures suggest that this dubious distinction may now belong to Nigeria). Among the BRICS (Brazil, Russia, India, China, and South Africa) countries, India has the lowest per capita income and Brazil continues to be competitive in nominal GDP. Additionally, other countries are not standing still; Indonesia and Mexico also aspire to grow ever faster.

Second, the reforms so far in India have been partial. There are still many "deep reforms" needed but require far more fortitude and could face much more resistance. The Modi government has carried out major reforms such as GST that unified India's markets and IBC to streamline the resolution process for non-performing assets (NPAs) in a time-bound manner. It even took the bold step of demonetization to curb India's shadow economy and bring many more individuals into the tax net, thus improving the tax revenue to GDP ratio which in turn increased the resources for investment in India's development.

The benefits of such reforms are already visible and should further boost the economy in the future. However, the need for further reforms in land, labor, agriculture, and trade policy is there but stymied by the opposition (regardless of which party is in power). Niti Aayog has estimated that India's growth rate could be boosted to 8-8.75 % from the currently projected 7-7.75 % by such reforms. While an incremental increase of 1% may look impressive, it will double the recent growth rate advantage of India versus China – much needed if India is to narrow the gap between the two economies.

Third, the nature of India's polity and society is such that only a transformational leader can make the breakthrough needed. Political incoherence and steadfast opposition to anything and everything characterize India's democracy (such may be the nature of democracy even though it is considered to be the best political system). Social schism based on religion, caste, and entrenched traditional practices continues unabated. The challenges are big, even if India's capacity to tackle them is equally big. The good news is that the Modi government has risen to the challenges; however, many of its initiatives have been stymied by the opposition due to the lack of a majority in the Upper House or strident opposition by vested interests. Therefore, the need for a strong government under a transformational leader is obvious: whether it will happen or not lies in the hands of the Indian people!

This page is intentionally left blank

Chapter **10**

Who Among India's Leaders Fits the Template of A Transformational Leader?

In this chapter, we comment on the transformational leaders of the past century cited earlier – Mustafa Kemal Ataturk, Franklin Delano Roosevelt, Lee Kuan Yew, Park Chung Hee, Deng Xiaoping, and Helmut Kohl as per the "template". Subsequently, we will look at three of India's post-independence leaders, Jawaharlal Nehru, Indira Gandhi, and Narendra Modi as to whether they can be considered transformational leaders.

When it comes to integrity, Ataturk's suppression of dissidents and personal foibles causes us to assign him a lower rank. Roosevelt's integrity is also questionable owing to his long-running affair with his secretary that came to light after his death, his efforts to pack the Supreme Court (that did not succeed), his manipulation of public opinions, and unfair treatment of the Japanese minority. Lee Kuan Yew's integrity is rated the highest, even though his succession first by his son and thereafter by handpicked successors does raise some questions. Park Chung Hee fought for the Japanese during

World War II and usurped power by suppressing opponents; therefore he did not get the highest rank for integrity. Helmut Kohl showed high integrity throughout his career but campaign financing scandals that came to light after he left the helm of his country's affairs have diminished his luster.

In any case, it is understandable that possessing and maintaining impeccable integrity while pursuing political power may be, perhaps, impossible. One can only expect some degree of shortcomings from even transformational leaders with high integrity.

The ability to connect with their followers, through oratory, speeches, writings, or personal gestures is critical to becoming a massively followed leader – transformational or otherwise. Both Ataturk and Roosevelt were powerful speakers; Roosevelt's inaugural address that Americans had nothing to fear except fear itself resonates even today and his fireside radio addresses were listened to with rapt attention by his followers.

In the same way, strategic thinking is critical for making the right choices. Every major decision has several options or alternatives: the final option taken will further influence other decisions down the road. While all of these leaders thought strategically, Lee Kuan Yew stands out because no one else could foresee the city-state of Singapore becoming the powerhouse that it is today. Ataturk was undeniably a military strategist, while Roosevelt along with Churchill dominated the strategic direction of the Allies during World War II. Park Chung Hee formulated South Korea's development strategy largely following Japan's export-oriented model but was astute enough to focus on electrification of the countryside, rural housing, and skill development to ensure the success of his strategy.

Nothing happens without successful implementation, and this is where many visionary leaders fail – their ideas run afoul of ground reality, or their implementation is either poorly managed or monitored. Achieving transformation requires the leader to be an effective manager with a sharp, eagle eye for details. They stand out by imposing their will on their followers and getting things done – through persuasion, manipulation, or even force, if necessary. Ataturk tolerated no opposition, Roosevelt charmed or manipulated his way throughout his administration, Lee Kuan Yew systematically promoted meritocracy to facilitate the execution of his programs, both Park Chung Hee and Deng Xiaoping kept the reins of power in their hands while advancing their protégés to positions of power, and Helmut Kohl managed international alliances and NATO to ensure that the reunification of Germany was possible.

However, successful execution invariably requires pragmatism; settling for the good versus insisting on the best is often the best choice, politics being an art and leverage for possibility. All these leaders showed pragmatism to a high degree: Lee Kuan Yew stood out in this regard, his policies shaped by trial and error. After first advocating for the union with Malaysia, he fell out with the central government, and Singapore was banished from the union. Thereafter, Lee Kuan Yew tried the statist, five-year plan for economic development before abandoning it for free-market, capitalist policies. Deng Xiaoping succeeded whereas Mao had failed due to his pragmatism as compared to Mao's dogmatic insistence on ideology.

The road to national transformation is never easy. There are many forks in the road: two steps forward and a step backward, even failure is sometimes inescapable. Many leaders can be derailed or sidelined by both foreseeable and unforeseen challenges; however, being able to make a comeback and relentlessly push on is what separates transformational leaders from their peers. Doggedness in pursuit of their goals, being resolute in the face of defeat, and resilience in making a comeback from adversity have been demonstrated by all of the leaders cited in this book. For example: Ataturk revived Turkey after the Ottoman Empire's defeat in World War I; Roosevelt led America out of the depression; Lee Kuan Yew built Singapore after it was thrown out of Malaysia; Park Chung Hee and Deng Xiaoping survived assassination attempts and political exile, and Helmut Kohl bounced back after electoral reverses.

The very nature of the transformation process is such that leaders are forced to think beyond the status quo or incremental change. They constantly learn from others and can "think out of the box". Ataturk went beyond the traditions of Islamic orthodoxy in his efforts to modernize Turkey; Roosevelt accepted hitherto untested Keynesian economic theory of using fiscal stimulus to revive the American economy; Lee Kuan Yew charted an entirely different course after his initial efforts to develop a statist, heavy-industry economy were not working and charted a very different course to turn Singapore into a global financial center and an attractive location for regional headquarters for multinationals; Deng Xiaoping was impressed by Singapore and created Shenzhen as testing ground for new policies based on the Singaporean model. Eventually, this led to the opening up of China to the world markets.

This capacity to learn, when combined with pragmatism, is essential for adopting as well as adapting policies to fit the changing circumstances in their respective countries. Undoubtedly, all of these leaders exhibit tireless energy in pursuit of their goals. Arguably, the outstanding example is that of Roosevelt who despite being incapacitated by polio, held the reins of power the longest among all American presidents and led the Allies to victory in World War II – which shaped the entire history of the world after this epochal event; Ataturk worked tirelessly to transform Turkey during his 15 years in power; Lee Kuan Yew led Singapore for 30 years and continued to be a mentor to his successors throughout his lifetime; Deng Xiaoping never completely let go until his death at the age of 93 even though he had resigned from his formal posts almost a decade earlier. Similarly, both Park Chung Hee and Helmut Kohl worked tirelessly until their careers were cut short by assassination and electoral defeats respectively.

We now turn to those of India's leaders post-independence, who can potentially be considered transformational leaders. Since independence in 1947, India has had 14 Prime Ministers, with seven having completed at least one term or more to make an impact sufficient enough to be considered whether it was transformatiorial or not. These seven are Jawaharlal Nehru, Indira Gandhi, Rajiv Gandhi, Narasimha Rao, Atal Bihari Vajpayee, Manmohan Singh, and Narendra Modi. While each of these made significant contributions to India's progress, we judge only three had an impact large enough to be considered transformational: Nehru, Indira, and Modi.

Nehru guided India's destiny for 17 years, laid the foundations for its democracy, built its new institutions, and was a leader of non-aligned nations. He was a committed

Fabian socialist in his economic ideology and an idealist in his foreign policy. While India progressed impressively under his watch, his lack of pragmatism led him to adopt a mixed economy model heavily influenced by the Soviet model whereby the "commanding heights" were state-controlled.

Similarly, his foreign policy did not emphasize self-interest sufficiently enough to see potential pitfalls: his faith in the newly created United Nations led him to believe that the Kashmir problem could be solved through its intervention, and his idealistic trust in China led him to creat policies inimical to India's interests – eventually culminating in India's defeat in the border war with China in 1962.

Indira Gandhi not only continued with Nehru's economic policies with a further tilt towards the Soviet Union but she also added populism to the mix, leading to the nationalization of banks, unrealistic "banish poverty" slogans, and imposition of tighter regulations on the economy, which culminated in the "emergency" that almost stifled India's democracy. Her pragmatism served her well both in pursuit of power and her signature achievement: enabling the creation of Bangladesh. Due to the unrealistic geopolitical construct of Pakistan with its two wings separated by 1500 miles, which was bound to fail, Indira mightily helped the process of Pakistan's disintegration through her support of the insurrection in favor of an independent Bangladesh – and by outmaneuvering the United States which sought to preserve the status quo. Since this required tilting towards the Soviet Union, an unintended consequence of her policies was a mindset in India that had rejected the adoption of the free-market economic policies of the West, even when these were being implemented in China.

As we have noted before, India began to change its economic policies under Rajiv Gandhi during the mid-1989s, followed by market reforms and the dismantling of the Licence Permit Raj under Narasimha Rao in 1991. The reform process was further accelerated under Atal Bihari Vajpayee, along with major initiatives to build India's infrastructure. Manmohan Singh's government continued such policies, buoyed by the worldwide economic boom in the mid-2000s during his first term.

Unfortunately, the financial crisis of 2008 followed by the Great Recession of 2008-09 led to unsustainable fiscal stimulus. This was further compounded by populist policies that almost brought the Indian economy to its knees – India went from being a bright spot among the BRIC (Brazil, Russia, India, China) bloc to the "Fragile Five" (Brazil, India, Indonesia, Turkey, Indonesia) – and high inflation. This was the context for the 2014 elections which brought Modi to the helm of affairs.

Modi had a demonstrated record of success with good governance and unprecedented economic growth in Gujarat during his 13 years (2001-14) as the Chief Minister. This resulted in the wide acknowledgment of his "Gujarat model", which eventually resonated with the electorate that gave him election wins in 2002, 2007, and 2012. Therefore, such a superb performance was expected of him as India's Prime Minister. However, what was not expected was his role as a social reformer and his success in foreign policy.

Indeed his opponents had questioned whether he had sufficient experience in foreign affairs, as this is mostly outside the purview of state governments. Modi has not only initiated social reforms through his "Swachh Bharat" or "Clean India" and "Beti Bachao, Beti Padhao" or "Save the Girl Child, Educate the Girl Child" campaigns but has added to India's prestige globally through popularizing Yoga and efforts to mitigate climate change.

The results of Modi's first term are extraordinary indeed – many polls of Indians acknowledge him as the best PM of India to date. We have summarized the performance metrics of his term versus others earlier to make out this case. As a matter of fact, the foundation of India's transformation has been laid – both due to Modi's efforts as well as that of his predecessors. At the same time, some observers have been disappointed; they had much higher, perhaps unrealistic, expectations.

They had expected deeper reforms, a faster rate of growth, and widespread privatization.

Perhaps, Modi was limited in what he could achieve in his first two terms because of his party's lack of majority in the Upper House; or being pragmatic, he resorted to incrementalism – with bolder reforms to come through if he gets another term. Modi certainly understands the need for a "New India" with "Reform, Perform, Transform" as his mantra. Given enough chance, possibly another 10 years, he may indeed become India's most transformational leader in history. At the moment, he is the only candidate likely to become such a leader, and yet his records to date are very much a "work in progress". None of the other contenders considered to be a feasible alternative (such as Rahul Gandhi, Mamata Banerjee, Akhilesh Yadav, and Mayawati) come close to him in most of the characteristics of transformational leaders. That the public feels the same way is a clear indication that Modi stands head and shoulders above any other leader when pollsters ask who is the most favored among India's leaders as PM.

Even within his own NDA, there are not many alternatives with the possible exception of Nitin Gadkari or Yogi Adityanath – speculative possibilities in the event that an alternative is needed if the current dispensation fails to get a majority in the forthcoming elections. Therefore, whether Modi gets to fulfill his articulated mission is very much an open question – the answer to which lies in the hands of India's electorate.

At the moment, pre-election polls indicate that there are three likely outcomes of the forthcoming elections: NDA returns with an absolute majority and Modi as PM, NDA does not get a majority but forms a coalition with support from other regional parties with someone other than Modi as PM, or the opposition comes to power in a coalition.

In the case of the first possibility, we can assume stability and continuity – with even bolder reforms and initiatives as the electorate would have reconfirmed Modi's mandate. In the second, while stability may be assured, continuity is less likely to occur due to the change at the top and the need to carry along the political coalition partners. Continued incrementalism is likely and the government will be cautious with respect to increasing the pace of reforms or undertaking new initiatives. The third possibility is the most problematic as far as India's transformation is concerned; opposition parties have yet to coalesce into a coherent and credible force with an alternative vision beyond "replace Modi, save democracy", and a common minimum program (or a manifesto) is yet to be articulated. There are no clear answers as to who will replace Modi or whether India's democracy indeed needs to be saved – given the current records of some Chief Ministers or the past "emergency" imposed by Indira Gandhi. The risk of a weak coalition either slowing down progress or regressing to the failed policies of the past is rather high with this possibility.

In a nutshell then, India's journey to prosperity – and possibly superpower status – is very much at a crossroads: it is apparent that transformation or regression is the main choice in front of the electorate in the coming elections!

The kind of leader India needs now to grow rapidly and sustain such economic miracles is someone who can stand up for the country when it is in grave danger. In recent history, COVID-19 shook every corner of the world and turned virtually everything upside down. COVID-19 was declared by the World Health Organization (WHO) as a global pandemic on March 11, 2020. India, as well as other nations, were seriously affected by the pandemic in huge, unimaginable ways – both personal and business activities were disrupted.

What is worth mentioning now is how India, against all odds, triumphed against the deadly COVID-19. Prime Minister Modi and his indefatigable team speedily inaugurated an almost non-contact telemedicine (e-health) system that streamlined the processes of identifying patients infected with the coronavirus, diagnosing them, treating and providing vaccines or prescription drugs to them without necessarily admitting all of them at the hospitals or clinics, and avoiding overcrowding and widespread transmission of the coronavirus. The patients were only asked to appear for tests at designated centers and their treatment was conducted remotely.

If India hadn't adopted an e-health system and encouraged the production of the Made-in-India COVID-19 vaccine, COVAXIN, designed by a collaboration between Bharat Biotech and the Indian Council of Medical Research (ICMR)-National Institute of Virology (NIV), the pandemic could have wreaked havoc in the country. In a spirit of friendship, India went ahead to make millions of COVAXIN available to other countries that urgently needed it, including Sri Lanka, Mauritius, Oman, Afghanistan, etc.

A transformational leader sees opportunity where others perceive difficulties and he isn't usually afraid to take a step further into a risky venture. Nearly 14 years after India's first lunar exploration spacecraft landed on the moon, Prime Minister Modi took up the challenge to continue the tradition of India's space exploration, elevating India among the comity of space-exploring nations such as the United States, Russia, the UK, China, etc. Indian lunar exploration mission, codenamed Chandrayaan, recorded another milestone on August 23, 2023, when its Chandrayaan-3 (the third in the series, and the second successful effort) landed safely on the moon's south pole.

Nation-building is pretty much like a ship – it takes a savvy, fearless captain to direct the course of a ship, irrespective of its size and how turbulent the oceans appear to be. There will always be storms and unfavorable weather to deal with, and it is the duty of a transformational leader to face all those obstacles without losing his enthusiasm. Being a global, multi-talented leader goes beyond partisan rhetoric. This is where a politician like Modi should be seen as a one-in-a-lifetime leader who comes on the scene to salvage our Indianness. For the first time ever, and chaired by Prime Minister Modi, India held the

G20 presidency for the year 2023. The G20 Summit is a group
of highly industrialized nations or fast-growing economies in
the world (a bloc that India comfortably fits in!) and, according
to the government, Modi is expected to use his tenure and the
platform to promote digital innovation, equitable access to
health globally, climate accountability, and all-encompassing
economic growth.

This unique opportunity gives Modi's government a rare
chance to broaden its *"Vasudhaiva kutumbakam"* philosophy,
which means that the *"The World is One Family"*. Soft-
power diplomacy is totally different from the aggressive
and antagonistic global politics that have created wars
and international conflicts among nations. Even his critics
would readily admit that Modi is reshaping India's foreign
policies in a positive way that emphasizes mutual respect and
partnerships.

Using the platform of G20 as its 2023 president, Modi did
not cower under Western influence to support the war that
has been raging on in Ukraine since Russia launched a large-
scale invasion of the country on February 24, 2022. Instead,
Modi appealed to the two warring parties to resolve their
conflict diplomatically. The same diplomatic independence was
displayed by him when he rejected to join the US and its allies
to frustrate Russia economically after Russia was accused by
the US of meddling in his presidential elections. This reveals
an interesting trend in the type of diplomacy Modi favors
– peaceful and harmonious partnership – something that is
very difficult for countries such as Japan and South Korea to
do because they always tag along with the US diplomatically.
Not making enemies could be viewed as an integral aspect

of Modi's Vishwamitra (global friend) outreach directed at enhancing India's geopolitical stature.

Modi's pro-women gestures could be seen in several gender-equality programs initiated under his dispensation. One of these policies is the "Beti Bachao, Beti Padhao Scheme" which was launched in 2015 and aimed at prohibiting female foeticide. More so, it promotes the girl child's education and protection, eliminating all forms of gender-based violence, and helping those who are vulnerable from being attacked in society. We can deduce that feeling safe and protected within our communities has probably encouraged an increasing number of Indian women to seek employment outside their matrimonial homes. A recent Ministry of Statistics and Programme Implementation survey (discussed in one The Economic Times' article) enumerated how girls and women who are 15 years old represented 30% of the labor force between 2019 and 2020 compared to 24.5% in 2018-19 and 23.3% in 2017-18 respectively. As expected, women's unemployment rate in India has plummeted in recent years from 5.6% in 2017-2018, 5.1% in 2018-2019 to 4.2% for 2019-20.

A consummate leader like Modi comes once in a century; since he assumed the prime ministerial office, he has his eyes set on transforming India's low-performing sectors while keeping or increasing the momentum for the fast-growing industries. It is like a destiny-imposed duty, and some of his contemporaries have praised him for his tireless efforts, most especially the way he focused on improving the lives of the poor. The Digital Benefit Transfer (DBT) program, geared at directly crediting less-fortunate beneficiaries of the government's subsidies, has been expanded by the Modi administration since the program was launched on January

1, 2013, by the Manmohan Singh government. Born into a disadvantaged caste and family himself, Modi understands what it takes to overcome poverty and earn a comfortable living. This is why he feels strongly for or constantly associates himself with the people working hard to make their lives and that of their families better.

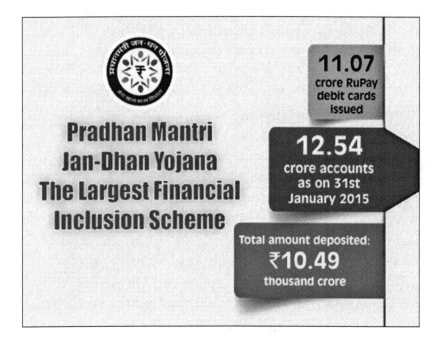

Chapter 11

The Dimensions of Political Transformations in India

Nation-building goes beyond just having a transformational leader; it equally involves reforming the political processes in the nation to engender stability and continuity of political relevance for the transformational leader.

It is an undeniable fact that no democracy in the world is perfect, including that of the United States where voting restriction or suppression is routinely perpetrated against minorities. There is also a grave concern about election fraud and an apparent lack of trust in elected US government officials. On record, the leading political party in Singapore, the People's Action Party (PAP), has held on to power for 63 years (since 1959), turning Singapore into a hegemonistic, one-party democratic state. Despite not being a liberal democracy, China's authoritarian one-party system runs itself like a democracy, but with some flaws, such as suppressing dissidents and religious intolerance. India has its own bunch of political challenges, which if left unresolved, could derail the current socioeconomic progress already achieved or make future aspirations to direct the country in the right course practically impossible.

In this chapter, we take a cognizant look at the different dimensions of Indian politics to highlight some sensitive, less-than-stellar aspects of it that require urgent and conscientious transformation so that India can be properly positioned on its way to becoming a superpower.

- **Elitist political class:** As one of the oldest democracies in the world, sadly enough, the Indian political class is still divided along regionalism and its caste systems. Even though most Indians associate themselves with one of the castes, the main concern is that despite the advancement in the Indian polity, people from other castes may still be unwilling to throw their absolute support behind politicians that do not belong to their castes or regions. Narendra Modi is reportedly from "Modh Ghanchi" in Gujarat, designated as the Other Backward Class (OBC) in India's caste system and it is just expected that Kshatriyas and Vaishyas, born rulers and masters of traders (many of their members are very rich and influential) could decide to mount stiff opposition against Modi's political continuation.

Unfortunately, this form of insular regionalism could derail existing progressive policies as people continue to be narrow-mindedly attached to their regions while neglecting the concept of "unity in diversity" and undermining national security as India hopes to present itself to the world as a unified country.

To be a formidable superpower, it is expedient for Indian people to shun anything that could divide them and embrace their diversities as a blessing. It must be remembered that the British exploited the perceptible divisions among people of the Old India to occupy the territories for 89 years, from 1858 to 1947. In the event that India's fortunes increase and it eventually becomes a superpower by virtue of its economic breakthroughs, it will still need a "One India" concept – people bound by one purpose and love for their nation – to defeat the enemies that may want to threaten it or its interests.

Extreme regionalism and casteism could have unintended consequences on the political process. For example, it could affect the total voter turnout during the general elections, and/ or it could make governing difficult for a prime minister who has very few people from his region or caste in the parliament since the other non-aligned politicians could simply rally around one another by forming a divisive opposition that could frustrate the prime minister's genuine efforts aimed at executing far-reaching, transformative reforms.

The history of India is, in certain ways, similar to that of America in the sense the American nationhood we see today wasn't usually like that when the Confederate States of America, comprising of the 11 Southern states, seceded from the Union in 1860-61 after alleging being treated unfairly like second-class citizens. India has its own history of secessionist or separatist movements; in the 1930s, there was the Khalistan Movement in the Punjab region calling for a separate state for the Sikhs. In 1967 in West Bengal, the Naxal-Maoist insurgents staged an armed rebellion to free themselves from the Indian Union, the group of Maoists who now organized themselves as the Communist Party of India. The essence of comparing India's past with that of America is to highlight the importance of building a nation on common patriotism. Otherwise, any schism among Indian people may hamper the country's bid for superpower status, because a nation that cannot hold its different parts together may soon fizzle out, like the Old USSR.

It is worth recognizing that Modi has taken decisive steps to unite Hindus under the "Hindutva" umbrella as part of his New India vision. Despite that, the caste, regionalism, and linguistic divisions persist and are exploited by opposition parties – as is being done by the I.N.D.I Alliance formed in 2023 to fight the 2024 elections. The Dravidian/Tamil secessionist movement continued as late as the 1960s and such sentiments are held even today by a minority. The North-Eastern had secessionist movements after India's independence, which have been largely resolved except Nagaland. The Khalistan Movement persists even today, most especially in the diaspora. These apparent divisions among the Indian populace call for a unifying agent – a leader who could impartially negotiate for peace across the aisle.

In a similar vein, China is not exempted from being affected by home-grown separatist movements or elements, because a host of dissident politicians in Hong Kong, Tibet, Taiwan, Inner Mongolia, and Xinjiang are not quite happy with their forceful marriage with mainland China. Should China ever fall into the trap of fighting with the United States, all the above-mentioned separatist states or regions would get a chance to betray China and opt-out as independent states. That is possibly the reason why the Chinese leadership never entertains the thought of going to war with the United States, because China is metaphorically sitting on a keg of gunpowder!

Therefore, India has a big job on its hands to bring everyone together under a unified nationhood, where every citizen can feel like they truly belong, and can pledge their undivided patriotism to the New India. The US can present a common front to its enemies because it has successfully sold nationalism to everyone and made it difficult for its enemies to infiltrate any perceived schisms among its people, which had long healed since the end of the American Civil War.

- **Women Empowerment:** As noticeable in several countries in Asia, Africa, Middle East, and South America, women empowerment, politically and economically, appears to be a total mirage. India is not exempted from this disturbing trend. Notably, 76 years after its independence, it is unimpressive to see that women are still hamstrung by restrictive patriarchy that makes women's political empowerment impossible in India. Apart from Mamata Banerjee, J. Jayalalithaa, and, of course, Indira Gandhi who became the first and only female prime minister in India, notably through her father's political connections, Indian women have been discouraged or unmotivated to actively participate in partisan politics.

Without a doubt, women remain the backbone of every national transformation, and ignoring their much-needed contributions at the regional, state, and national levels would make complete nation-building impossible or cause the vision to drag endlessly for years to the point that it may become unrealizable. The Modi government shocked the world and even the local pundits when he elected 11 female ministers to his second-term cabinet, which represented the highest number of women in an Indian government in 17 years.

According to the World Bank, women represent 48.8% of India's population (2022). It indicates that women could exert a huge influence on every area of the nation-building processes, from mobilizing themselves, their families, and associates to actively participating in electioneering to sacrificing their time and resources to wholeheartedly support national transformational activities, in as much as they understand it would benefit them, their children, and the generations unborn.

In its 2023 Global Gender Inequality Gap Report which measures how countries incorporate health, economic, and political empowerment for their women, The World Economic Forum ranks India 127th out of the 140 nations on the list. China ranked 107th, while Japan ranked 125th. It can be deduced from the statistics above that nations have to deliberately empower their women to make them participate productively in nation-building. Despite being richer than China, Japan has historically (and unwilling to change this pattern) driven their women to the backstage. In Japan's Kishida administration, there are only two female ministers, and the same trend is noticeable in both public and private industries where men mostly cling to the leadership of those establishments. Similarly, China has dropped on the scale, from being ranked 63rd in 2006 to 107th in 2023 – this figure could only be indicative of the worsening disempowerment of Chinese women, who are not frequently featured in China's male-dominated political class.

It takes a transformative leader like Modi to identify the potential of Indian women. Men may hold the baton of power, but they cannot solely direct the affairs of the country if women remove their needful support. So, instead of perceiving them as a second-class citizen to be pushed backstage, why can't leaders in the regions and states emulate Modi's good example and give Indian women a chance to lead politically? We understand this may appear to be a hypothetical question, but if India is vying to outpace America and other superpowers, it must ditch the belief that men should always be in the driver's seat. It is like the head of a family saying his wife is not important, and so her efforts are not needed. That's a myopic way to build a home or a nation, and it is time those at the helm of affairs formulate women-friendly policies to bring Indian women to the center of power.

Another indication of Modi's intention to accord women their rights and freedom was seen in his involvement in the Triple Talaq case. Before the act was declared unconstitutional by the Indian Supreme Court on August 22, 2017, the Hanafi Sunni Muslims could simply divorce their wives by merely shouting the word "talaq" (the Arabic word for "divorce") three times. This shouting of the word "talaq" could also be transmitted orally, electronically, or in writing. Modi's aspiration to create an environment of gender equality, justice, and commonwealth for all Indians under the country's Uniform Civil Code (Article 44) motivated him to openly support the Indian Supreme Court's decision.

- **Corruption in Politics:** A recent study reportedly claimed that developing countries, including India, lose an astonishing amount to corruption every year, estimated to be worth about $1 trillion. To be honest, this is a lot of money that could have been invested in nation-building but slipped away through political corruption which has failed to enact laws against illegal capital flight.

According to Global Financial Integrity, India is one of the top five countries, including China, Malaysia, Mexico, and Russia that lost about $35 billion to illegal money flows yearly. Most of the illegally transferred funds ended up in tax havens where India has no prerogative authority or jurisdiction to impose the appropriate taxes on them. With decreasing revenues, the Indian government will have no apparent option but to keep cutting spending on areas that should have been developed, such as education, health, and other sectors of the economy.

The main cause of these financial woes can be attributed to the failure of the political class to overhaul or reform the necessary laws guiding business activities in the country. When politicians rig elections to get into political positions, one can expect that they will look the other way when accountable actions are required of them. This is also happening in the United States where politicians collect huge donations from corporations and shy away from supporting legislation that may hurt their generous corporate donors.

It is no longer news that elected political officials are fond of abusing their honorable posts, stealing from the government by inflating contracts, taking bribes, and perverting justice for personal aggrandizement. This is a common plague in most nations where their political parties are merely the bedrock of political corruption. The negative effect of this is that the electorate will simply lose interest in the governing process when their leaders cannot be trusted; people will fail to participate in elections or even rally behind a transformational leader.

Corruption in high places – in governmental offices and among elected government officials – is still a hydra-headed monster that India is fighting with all its might. By shunning corruption and embracing accountability, Prime Minister Modi has positioned himself to be the best candidate to help India overcome the debilitating impacts of corruption, nepotism, and appeasement that might have been holding the country back. This is a common social problem in many nations, and political corruption can become a real obstacle to progress.

On his 10th Independence Day address, Modi made a strong case against political corruption and called for "probity, transparency, and impartiality", factors he believed would turn India into a great nation by 2047. Modi posited that *"corruption, nepotism (parivaarvad), and appeasement were 'evils' pulling the country backward"*.

The Transparency International, an independent watchdog that monitors corruption in many nations ranked India 85th out of 180 nations. Delivering him from the ramparts of the Red Fort, Prime Minister Modi reminded Indian people that they are capable, courageous, and hardworking, but *"the only hurdle that could come in the way of the country's development is 'corruption, dynastic politics, and appeasement'*, referring to some *"bad elements"* that had remained an active part of Indian politics and social order for the past 75 years.

Instead of exuding an elitist aura and acting snobbishly toward lowly people, Modi's Hindutva philosophy emphasizes "satisfaction for all without appeasement of any", and his nationalism, development, and social welfare policies are the bases India needs now for its transformation.

- **Mainstreaming politics:** Another thing the Modi government deserves genuine praise for is its efforts in mainstreaming politics in India. In addition to having the largest number of female ministers in his administration, according to a World Values Survey, it was revealed that up to 50% of Indian youths now classified themselves as "very" or "rather" interested in politics since 1990. Gone are the days when politics in India was all old people's affairs. The Indian youths have realized that they have a significant role to play in transforming their country. They could help identify and throw their unwavering support behind a transformational leader they know could better their lives. We have seen an example of this in the United States in 2008 when 66% of young people under the age of 30 voted massively to bring Barack Obama to the presidency. They exercised their electoral rights and caused an unprecedented shift in American politics by supporting a black presidential candidate, something that might not have been achievable without their great support.

If India is going to rule the world, it must actively encourage its young people to play a significant part in politics. This would require the youths to be advised to shun political violence and vie for elective positions where they could learn how to govern. The future of any country lies on the shoulders of its young people. If the older politicians continue to believe that they would live forever or be in power forever, there is no grander self-delusion than that. However, if they take it upon themselves to liberalize politics, too, and make it attractive to young people and women to participate in, they are inadvertently preparing a bright future for India.

I.N.D.I.A.: Exploring the Potency of the Opposition Alliance

I.N.D.I.A. is an acronym for the name chosen by the staunch opposition to Prime Minister Modi's Bhartiya Janata Party (BJP). I.N.D.I.A stands for Indian National Development Inclusive Alliance. It is an opposition comprising 26 different political parties; it was the former Indian National Congress-led United Progressive Alliance (UPA) that is being rebranded as I.N.D.I.A.

I.N.D.I.A was founded to counter the BJP-led National Democratic Alliance (NDA). It is obvious that the opposition's goal is to stop Prime Minister Modi from winning the next general election slated for 2024. How well-coordinated are they? And what is the possibility that they can eventually succeed in unseating Modi?

To find plausible answers to the questions above, it may be sensible to analyze the performances of UPA's past two governments under Manmohan Singh and their apparent failures as documented in some literature. Since UPA rebrands itself as I.N.D.I.A, Indian people would not, in a flash, forget the disappointments and the chaotic dispensations the former UPA had pushed them through, from 2004 to 2014 when the alliance was in power. It may appear naïve for anyone to expect that a simple name change may do the magic for UPA, as Indian people won't quickly forget UPA's mistakes as detailed below:

The truth remains that the Manmohan Singh's government should be praised for putting India on the path of economic liberalization; however, his administration did commit some errors that have not completely disappeared from average Indian electorates' minds, such as:

1. **Uncompleted Rural Electricity Projects:** Even until he completed his second term in office, the Manmohan Singh government didn't complete the rural electrification projects they had started. One could see power lines connected across 5.6 lakh villages, but no power or electricity is running through them. This colossal failure could be attributed to poor management of the state electricity board during his tenure. That

mistake alone left India reeling from high fuel prices and pollution from generating electricity from coal.

2. **The Unique Identity Project:** The UPA government initiated the Unique Identity Project, but it remained unfinished by the time the dispensation was replaced by Modi. It was the Modi government that eventually rolled out the full scope of the project, providing legal backing for the project through the passage of the Aadhaar (Targeted Delivery of Financial and other Subsidies, Benefits, and Services) Act 2016 on March 3, 2016.

3. **Inadequate Reforms and Corruption:** Most pundits still believed that the Manmohan Singh government could have done more by giving India the necessary reforms it needed to maintain and expand its economic growth recorded during the Congress reign but the governmental procedures were carried out slowly and sometimes in a chaotic manner. The Manmohan Singh government's approaches to national issues became even more shoddy after accusations of political and economic corruption were levied against it. Manmohan Singh himself refused to appear before the Joint Parliamentary Council that had invited him in April 2013 to clear the air about his involvement in the 2G corruption case.

4. **Unfinished Foreign Policies:** Manmohan Singh, the last leader of UPA, made several promises and attempts to forge a new foreign relations trajectory for India, but his inability to see each planned agreement or proposed partnership through almost cost him his mandate when his efforts to hurriedly signed a US-India Civil Nuclear Deal, which was roundly rejected by the opposition and some members of UPA, fell through.

If UPA is indeed serious about kicking the BJP out of governance, why hadn't it done so in the past two general elections? It is generally believed that UPA and, of course, I.N.D.I.A lacks internal cohesion. The alliance's officers might be putting up appearances at political rallies or on campaign grounds, but their marriage seems shaky and hastily drawn up just in time for the 2024 general election. The 26 parties that are members of I.N.D.I.A have non-negotiable and party-specific ideologies that are wide apart. This seemingly makes it difficult for them to produce a central sociopolitical message that could rival that of the BJP.

The Indian National Congress (INC) is not a stranger to being part of an alliance that would later crumble. Based on a news report in 2009, UPA and its main members noticed that their alliance was ill-prepared to depose Modi due to its shallow structure which made it impossible to have tentacles in strategic regions or states across India. This was the backdrop that had led to the birth of the new alliance, I.N.D.I.A. which in itself cannot boast of being cohesive at the center. This apparent lack of ideologically similar political aspirations seems to weaken the alliance and makes it appear like its collapsing predecessor, UPA.

On their part, the leadership of the BJP-led National Democratic Alliance (NDA) has dismissed I.N.D.I.A as another attempt by the elitist party, the Indian National Congress (INC) to cajole people into voting it into power in the 2024 general election. Guru Prakash Paswan, the BJP party spokesperson said, "They are not concerned about the nation's development or any other interest of the nation. The only thing that unites them is the lust for power, corruption, and dynasty. That is the important thread."

Due to his sterling performance as a two-term prime minister, Modi has consequently raised the bar about what transformative qualities the next prime minister of India should display or embody. Indian people may be unwilling to elect any political officials who could end up slowing down the country's current socioeconomic progress, those who may unwittingly take the country back to the Dark Ages.

What happens in 2024 is in the hands of the Indian electorates – they could either decide to keep Modi in power and watch him advance India towards superpower status or take a risk bringing in another, untested leader that may wind back all the economic progress made so far. As it turns out, the 2024 general election will be the litmus test for India's economy's chance of survival, expansion, and further transformation.

Chapter 12

What the Indian Populace Stands to Gain from Far-Reaching Socioeconomic Reforms

When a nation prospers it is its citizens that will immensely benefit from the largesse. Since the economic liberalization and high-growth performance that began in the early 1990s in India, the country has been able to achieve one of the most sought-after economic developments by many developing nations – expanding its middle class.

1. **Expanding Middle-Class:** It is a fact that India's ever-expanding middle class holds the key to their country's recent, never-seen-before economic performance as their household incomes and purchasing power spiked dramatically. According to the People Research on India Consumer Economy (PRICE) ICE 3600 surveys that were calculated utilizing primary data, it is deduced that the Indian middle class has been growing steadily at a rate of 6.3% annually between 1995 and 2021. At the moment, India's middle class is estimated to be about 31% of the entire country's population, and this number is projected to reach 38% by 2031 and 60% in 2047 respectively,

exactly when India will be celebrating its centenary since its independence.

Due to their higher incomes and a habit of discretionary spending, India's middle class can be credited for creating new, big markets that are currently responsible for increased domestic consumption. As a result of this, this class has the hidden economic power to turn India's SMEs into gigantic, global brands that could become attractive to foreign investors who want to profit from the burgeoning, local consumption powerhouse.

Table 11.1   India's Growing Prosperity (2023)

Consuming class	Income class (Rs. '000 at 2020-21 prices)	Number of households ('000)		Annual growth in households between 2015-16 to 2020-21 (%)
		2015-16	2020-21	
Destitute	<125	46,474	45,171	-0.6
Aspirers	125-500	1,55,984	1,60,792	0.6
Seekers	500-1,500	61,140	77,128	4.8
Strivers	1,500-3,000	10,117	13,799	6.4
Near Rich	3,000-5,000	2,286	3,263	7.4
Clear Rich	5,000-10,000	2,024	3,171	9.4
Sheer Rich	10,000-20,000	1,495	2,431	10.2
Super Rich	>20,000	1,057	1,807	11.3
	Total	2,80,576	3,07,563	1.9

Source: The Economic Times (2023)

The table above shows promising progress in how Prime Minister Modi's economic policies and those of his immediate predecessors are pulling average Indians out of poverty. The figures indicate a systematic reduction in the number of households enmeshed in abject poverty over five years by 0.6%, and the number of sheer rich and super-rich, within the same period, increased by 10.2% and 11.3% respectively. The simplest way to interpret this data is to affirm that Indian households are getting richer every year, taking advantage of the prevailing, streamlined economic policies to increase their net worth.

This interesting trend should continue in the next 5-10 years if a leader like Modi is allowed to continue his socioeconomic reforms. Moreover, it is expected that with tangible disposable income at their disposal, India's middle class could comfortably afford to send their children to good schools thereby raising highly educated, future leaders for the country.

Over time, one would expect the routine religious and sociocultural strife, which is often attributed to poverty, to subside as the middle class focuses more on gratifying discussions and interests, such as supporting local businesses to thrive and helping their nation to become great. With robust industrial growth and the existence of high-paying jobs in the urban areas, migration from one region to the other will occur and, over time, extreme regionalism will fade away. This can result in a groundbreaking shift in India's sociocultural order whereby people begin to perceive anywhere they could find well-paying jobs and live a better life as their "home". In essence, this could lead to an unplanned unification experience where all Indian people start to purely see one another as brothers and sisters rather than looking at one another through the lens of casteism and regionalism.

Due to their consumption of foreign goods and services, India's rich middle class has helped spawn entirely new kinds of industries. Today, foreign companies such as Apple, Inc. and other tech companies are flocking to India, opening offices in the country, and moving their production from China to India. In the course of this modern business revitalization, the Indian startup ecosystem is fast-growing as foreign investors or entrepreneurs fly in with their money to fund or invest in these new, young enterprises. Some of them have gone on to become unicorns, which is a term for companies with at least $1 billion in valuations (or market capitalization); in fact, there are currently 38 unicorns in India. This rare and very important industrial development further puts pressure on the Indian government to reform India's economy to give those young India's startups a level playing field with either their local or foreign rivals. As of 2021, there were 39,000 startups in India, employing over 470,000 people.

2. **Digitization:** The concept of "Digital India" was launched by the Modi government, and it aims to establish transparency in governance through e-government as well as streamlining business activities in the private sector. With this cashless or contactless technology, it has become relatively easier for people to obtain government forms or apply for licenses/ permits online. They can also pay taxes online and avoid lengthy travels to governmental offices to do the same. This could also be used as a process for

accountability as most statistics or information about government's activities – those in public databases that were previously inscrutable – can now be accessed or even downloaded without experiencing any hindrances or delays known for paper-based applications. In the health sector, e-medical reports have been replacing paper ones, making it possible for people to obtain, store, and transfer their medical reports from one hospital to another to be treated without any delay.

In the private sector, mostly in banking and other financial services, digitalization ensures that digital payment solutions are supported, and businesses and consumers can make transactions quickly and safely. The Unified Payments Interface (UPI) developed by the National Payment Corporation of India necessitated that real-time payments be securely processed in seconds. In Fiscal Year 21, it was reported that UPI processed 22.3 billion transactions that has a total value of Rs 41 trillion. The transactions increased to 46 billion in 2022, with an estimated value of Rs 84 trillion. It is not surprising that local micro, small, and medium enterprises (MSMEs) benefited the most because 87.3 percent of the 41.4 lakh transactions that were carried out across the MSME ministry were executed digitally.

Digitalization opens the rare door for retail investors to try their hands on creating wealth for themselves. It was reported that about 10.7 million Demat accounts were operated by them between April 2020 and January 2021, propelling the Indian stock markets to an unprecedented $3 trillion market capitalization in 2021.

India's financial institutions take advantage of the digitalization process to develop many banking solutions for their customers, who include local farmers and petty traders, facilitating loan applications and disbursement. Now, farmers can get paid quickly and timely reinvest their returns in their farms, growing them steadily to the point that many of them have embraced export-oriented international trades made possible by online marketplaces such as China's Alibaba, America's Amazon, and Japan's Rakuten. It is not rare today to see a local farmer somewhere in India exporting his products across the globe and getting paid electronically and quickly. Credit must be given to whom it is due – if the Modi government had chosen not to toe the line of the free-market economy that was started by his predecessors, India wouldn't have a chance to compete globally as it is doing right now.

3. **Telecommunication/Communication:** Since it was liberalized in the 1990s alongside other strategic industries, India's telecommunication sector has grown significantly to the point that it is now playing a tangible role in the country's socioeconomic development. Based on the projection by the India Brand Equity Foundation (IBEF), India's telecommunications industry should reach a market size of $46.39 billion by 2024, because it has been growing at a Compound Annual Growth Rate (CAGR) of 7.16% year-on-year.

With 1179.49 million subscribers, India's telecom industry is the second largest in the world by number of telephone users – when putting both fixed and mobile phones into consideration. There is no doubt that the telecommunication sector is instrumental in encouraging transparency in governance with the introduction of e-governance. In the same way, it has helped bridge the gap between the urban and rural settlements as people could easily make calls on their mobile phones to connect with their loved ones and/or business associates anywhere in India or overseas.

One important aspect of the telecom liberalization undertaken by the Modi government is that it makes the sector attractive to foreign direct investors as well as foreign telecom companies that come to operate in India. So, in 2020-2021, the telecom sector contributed about 6% to India's GDP, and this is projected to expand at a CAGR of 9.4%, most especially from 2020 to 2025. Some of the factors contributing to the industry's full-throttle growth include but are not limited to favorable regulations or reforms, increased accessibility, the introduction of Mobile Number Portability (MNP), low prices, expansion of 3G, 4G, and 5G coverage, and the ever increasing demand for telephony and mobile internet.

4. **Made in India:** From being a global agricultural powerhouse to a fast-growing industrial giant, India has always been a force to reckon with in Asia and every other part of the globe. There are Made-in-India products everywhere; you can see them on supermarket shelves in Europe, Africa, the Americas, etc. When Indian automobiles and tractors are shipped to overseas markets, some of which are manufactured in

partnerships with other global automobiles such as KIA,
Nissan, Volkswagen, Renault, Hyundai, etc., or designed
locally, they are warmly accepted by consumers because
of their toughness and good quality. There are Indian
electronics, footwear, machines, etc., and lately Indian
software and IT products.

As India gradually shifts to an export-oriented market
economy, one would expect more and more Indian
products to hit the international markets. The good news
about this development is that Indian businesses, large
and micro, and Small and Medium Enterprises (MSMEs)
can earn foreign exchange. India has already put in place
policies that would support smooth international trade
payment systems. The more foreign exchange Indian
local businesses could earn, the better it is for their
operations and the more workers would be employed by
them.

The Made-In-India Campaign gets more impetus
from the Modi administration when compared with
his predecessors. The numbers don't lie – highlighted
below are some statistics that could be verified in the
public domain to show how Modi has given maximum
assistance or incentives to Indian companies and spurred
more growth in manufacturing and other industries since
he assumed office.

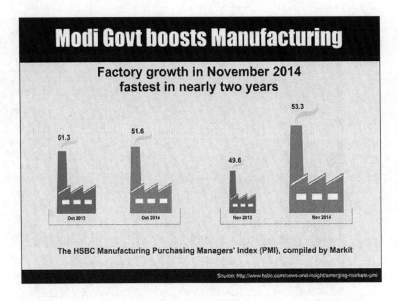

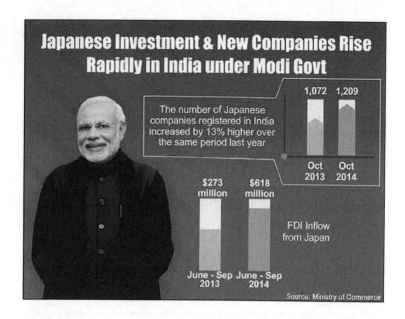

Investors spellbound by Modi magic

The DSP BlackRock India Investor Pulse Survey results reflect very high levels of optimism and positivity among Indian Investors

81% feel positive about their financial future against a global average of just 56%

54% say that the job market is improving against a global average of just 21%

56% feel that the economy is getting better against a global average of just 22%

Source: http://www.dspblackrock.com/

5. **Infrastructural Developments:** It is emblematic of transformational leadership to focus on developing essential infrastructure that could engender or support the growth of all economic sectors in a country. We can all witness how the Modi government is massively investing in infrastructure that India requires to expand on or at least maintain its current growth rate.

Between 2014 and 2023, India's infrastructural development has been boosted by Modi's readiness and ability to execute several developmental, high-cost projects simultaneously. During the period of his reign, India added over 53,000 kilometers of national highways, thereby increasing rural road connectivity coverage to about 99% through the Pradhan Mantri Gram Sadak, which is a landmark achievement. By calculation, this roughly puts the pace of highway construction at about 37 km per day.

Another dimension of India's structural development and expansion is its railway networks. The Modi government oversees the doubling of train lines as well as the Railway's electrification. Most importantly, the manufacturing of the Vande Bharat Express takes center stage – which is the first "Made-in-India" semi-high-speed train. So far, 41 Vande Bharat trains are currently running, and another 400 Vande Bharat express trains are due for manufacturing by 2026.

A total of 20 cities can now be reached by the metro rail systems, giving people more transportation and directly easing traffic congestion within those cities. It is estimated that about 22 million people use trains in India per day. That alone is about four times the entire population of Singapore.

The Modi government has also made significant advancements in aviation. The UDAN Project is aimed at increasing the number of commercial-level airports at several locations within the country. In the last nine years, 74 new airports have been constructed and they are operational. To encourage FDI in aviation, the Modi government has reformed the sector by allowing up to 100% FDI ownership for non-scheduled air transport services and regional air transport services through automatic routes. For helicopter and seaplane services, up to 100% FDI is also allowed through the automatic route.

Concerning India's waterways, a total of 111 waterways in the country have been declared as National Waterways, putting them under the direct management of the central government. Due to the volume of passengers and cargo that utilize India's waterways every year, it becomes important for them to be properly managed and channeled. In 2017-2018, the waterways handled about 55 million tons (55 MT) of cargo, which eventually increased to 72 MT in 2018-2019. The significant jump in the tonnage of cargo plying India's waterways could be considered as a measure of increase in productivity as well as expansion in the size of overseas markets open to Made-in-India goods.

Other equally important infrastructures that the Modi-led government has constructed in India include the World's highest railway bridge, the Atal Tunnel (the World's longest tunnel), the Chenab Bridge, and several other projects such as the Eastern and Western Peripheral Expressway, Saryu Nahar Irrigation Canal, and so on.

6. **Employment:** The post-COVID 19 indicators reveal that the Indian employment state has been rebounding. It is clear that the Modi government's strong macroeconomic processes have overall strengthened the Indian economy to the point that there are various channels for job creation, which include the rising employment by Indian startups and the availability of job opportunities via new career paths such as in data analytics, AI, automation, machine learning, cloud computing, etc.

Interestingly enough, the jump in Employees' Provident Fund Organization (EPFO) subscriptions indicates that more and more Indian businesses are becoming formalized, which is amazing because the government could tag those businesses to pay their appropriate taxes and consequently increase revenues. Before now, owing to the non-formalization of India's small businesses, several were not paying their due taxes. In November 2021 alone, it was reported that the monthly total new EPF subscriptions were 13.95 lakh – this represented the highest figure in any given month since 2017, amounting to about 109.21 percent growth in EPF subscriptions. It is equally impressive that the Unemployment Rate (UR), the Labour Force Participation Rate (LFPR), and the Worker Population Rate (WPR), according to the Periodic Labour Force Survey Data, have almost returned to their pre-COVID-19 levels by the last quarter of 2020-2021.

The Modi-led government's socioeconomic policies have contributed immensely to job creation across all sectors. Most especially, the Make-in-India Campaign that offers several incentives for India's businesses has indirectly increased the number of employment opportunities created by those businesses. The incentives include tax exemptions, infrastructure support, access to technology, easy access to land and financing, and productive regulatory procedures.

7. **Pension Scheme:** While the Employees' Provident Fund Organization (EPFO) organizes the pension scheme for employees of private enterprises, the Defined Contribution-based New Pension System (NPS), which began on January 1, 2004, provides a pension for government employees. Efforts have been deployed towards making sure that Indian people have something, in the form of a pension, to fall back on after retiring from work. The Modi government has also been taking the necessary steps to ensure that all eligible Indian workers are covered.

According to the 2011 census, only about 12% of India's total workforce (about 58 million people) is covered under various pension schemes. Those who are covered individuals work for the organized sectors and are employed by the private and public sector enterprises, government, and government enterprises, public and private sector enterprises, compulsorily covered by the Employees Provident Fund Organization (EPFO), as employers that have 20 or more employees are expected to subscribe to EPFO.

However, about 88% of India's workforce is employed in the unorganized sector like being self-employed, farmers, daily wage workers, etc. and others who work for the organized sector but are not compulsorily covered by the EPFO could enjoy some level of coverage under the traditional Public Provident Fund (PPF) and Postal Saving Schemes. And the Modi government has been exploring avenues for making sure India's workers' pensions and savings are properly disbursed to them when they eventually retire from active duties.

Rebranding India: A Critical Look at the Possible Benefits of Indian Sociocultural Revitalization

Considering the current situation in India, even the most optimistic experts believe it would be a very tough task to formulate a cultural policy that would be generally acceptable to all Indian people. There is a cogent reason for this proposition: India is so culturally, religiously, politically, and socially diverse that any attempt to disrupt the status quo by introducing an unfavorable sociocultural revitalization policy may elicit unexpected reactions, albeit violent from different quarters. The most important question is: Can India continue to exist in its current partially unified state as it aspires to become a superpower? The answer to this sensitive question may be complicated!

At least, one could expect India's new sociocultural order to be in line with Mahatma Gandhi's ardent hope when he said, *"to safeguard democracy, the people must have a keen sense of independence, self-respect and their oneness, and should insist on choosing as their representatives only such persons as are good and true."* The emphasis from the quote above is on "oneness" which could only be achieved when politicians of noble character and accountability are chosen to represent the people. Once again politics, as an art, surprisingly has the power to transform any nation if it is played fairly and in an all-encompassing manner.

The New India requires a new blueprint for its sociocultural revitalization, and it turns out that the one that could pass the test of being wholeheartedly accepted by everyone in the country must be enshrined in the existing Indian Constitution tenets that promote *"justice, liberty, oneness, and equality for all citizens."*

Human cultures are bigger than a mere combination of rituals, traditions, signs, symbols, and fashion – they are equally a representation of people's identities and communal values. Any cultural policy that must be designed and eventually implemented in India must recognize the fact that people would be willing to defend their identities and values if they are misrepresented, undermined, and/or abolished. A sociocultural policy that could work for India must be the one that convinces all stakeholders that their communal, regional, or state interests and identities would be respectfully represented.

Let's return again to Mahatma Gandhi and tap from his great wisdom about how India's cultural policy should be formulated. On April 5, 1936, in a conference at Allahabad, Gandhi gave his ever-riveting advice about how to promote sociocultural harmony among Indian people despite the prevailing cultural differences. He said, *"Many of us are striving to produce a blend of all the cultures which seems today to be in clash with one another. No culture can live if it attempts to be exclusive. There is no such thing as pure Aryan Culture in existence in India Today. Whether the Aryans were indigenous to India or were unwelcome intruders, does not interest me much. What does interest me is the fact that my remote ancestors blended with one another with the utmost freedom and we of the present generation are the result of that blend."* The "blend" that was in existence centuries ago among Indians' ancestors is what the Modi dispensation is trying to emulate, despite living in a modern world with complex and sometimes confusing expectations from all stakeholders.

Here are some important determinants for success that the Modi government has been incorporating into Indian nationhood to implement a true and lasting cultural revitalization policy that will satisfy all people:

1. **National character:** The concept of "National Character" stems from the efforts to offer a convincing answer to the all-important question: *"What does it mean to be an Indian?"* It is certain that different Indians would proffer diverse answers to the same question, based on their

individualistic Indian experience. But this is not what national character is all about.

National character, in essence, depicts an ideology of collective experience, mindset, feeling, and behavior expected of people residing in a country. As a culturally diverse setting, and through its globally renowned Bollywood, India has successfully exported its common-cause cultural activities and behaviors to the world. By merely watching Indian films and dramas, non-Indians could quickly identify or understand that Indian cultures are family-based, with their sets of written and unwritten social rules and values. That could be described as part of Indian national character, but does that mean every Indian acts the way it is shown in Bollywood films? Certainly not!

According to the 2011 national census, it was indicated that Hindus made up 79.8% of the Indian population, while Muslims were 14.2%, Christians 2.3%, and Sikhs 1.7% respectively. If there is going to be a national character that is well-received by all Indian people, it should embrace the attributes of all religions in the country, or at least, the main religions. The way religion is made part and parcel of cultures in this modern world shows that a person may feel disenfranchised if his/her religion is obliterated.

An article in Time Magazine highlighted the main reasons why most people perceive Modi as a great unifier of the Indian people: his genuine efforts at creating good policies for all to thrive and succeed in their respective callings; his promotion of peaceful co-existence among

Indians of different regions, castes, religions, etc.; his willingness to encourage women and youths to actively participate in politics and matters leading to socioeconomic transformation. Giving people what they need, both material resources and legal support, caused Indian people to admire Modi and his approaches to governance. As his second-term tenure rolls to an end, the enthusiasm or excitement he has created in the populace over these past nine years is unabated, and his plan to project an amazing national character for all Indian people is pretty much a work in progress.

2. **Cultural legitimacy:** As quoted above, Mahatma Gandhi bared his mind on the sensitive subject of cultural legitimacy. He said, *"No culture can live if it attempts to be exclusive. There is no such thing as pure Aryan Culture in existence in India Today. Whether the Aryans were indigenous to India or were unwelcome intruders, does not interest me much."* This means that politics should never be employed to undermine people's cultures, as is done in the West. For the most part, cultural acculturation or assimilation, a Western cultural ideology, expects the newly arrived immigrants to throw away their own cultures and wholly accept their host countries' mannerisms. However, the New India Modi is envisaging and elevating its emblematic of the total of cultures and religions within its jurisdiction. This is how a new cultural rebirth that is considerate, flexible, peaceful, and suitable to everyone can be designed for the New India.

3. **Homogeneity (Unity in Diversity):** When the government establishes fairness among its citizens, as the

Modi government is doing, people will naturally respond in kind by being loyal followers and supporters. Since he assumed office, Prime Minister Modi has taken it upon himself to resolve some difficult religious and cultural conflicts that had happened during his dispensation. The idea of homogeneity is not for any Indian to reject their own intricate cultures or religions, it is all about peacefully occupying the same space while exhibiting a great level of flexibility and mutual respect for each other's cultural orientation.

Unlike in Japan where nearly 98% of the people are homogeneously Japanese, India, according to Mahatma Gandhi, could create a peaceful cohabitation among its citizens where no one raises the divisive question of the other's ancestral origin, as it has been proved beyond reasonable doubt that all Indians came from different sources but they could be "One People" under a new kind of arrangement proposed and implemented by a unifying transformational leader.

Modi took a decisive step to unify all Indian states and unions under one constitutional umbrella and oversee the abrogation of Article 370. Until its abrogation, Article 370 gave the Assembly of the State of Jammu and Kashmir the unique rights, between 1952 and 2019, to draft its own constitution and self-rule itself. Now, divided into two unions – Jammu and Kashmir in the west and Ladakh in the east, these two unions are governed by the central government using the legislations that are applicable to all Indian citizens.

It is important to consider this move in a positive way; the former State of Jammu and Kashmir used to live separately on their own and seemed like they, who are mostly Muslims, were socio-politically cut off from mainland India. However, integrating them within the Indian Constitution affirms egalitarianism, justice, and oneness and reveals how Modi is making peaceful overtures to Indians of all religious affiliations, brokering long-lasting peace.

4. **Spiritual and Cultural Rebirth:** The Modi government's decision to redevelop the Central Vista has been dubbed "Modi's New India Policy". It is an honest attempt to keep the memories of India's past administrations alive for generations unborn to know how the nation, also known as Bhārat, came into existence. The Central Vista project involves renovating the monuments and buildings erected during the British Rule, as well as the Parliament House, Presidential Garden, North and South Block, and National Museum of India.

On August 5, 2020, Prime Minister Modi graced the ground-breaking ceremony for the construction of Ram Mandir, which is a Hindu Temple dedicated to Ram Lalla. It is worth noticing that the successive governments in India, beginning from Rajiv Gandhi to others, have been in one way or the other involved with the construction of the Ram Temple, but none of them could execute the project for different reasons. Over the years, the project became quite controversial, at one point causing violent and deadly inter-religious clashes between the Muslims and Hindus, and a 2019 Indian Supreme Court judgment recommended that the construction of the Ram Temple be organized as a trust and handed over to the Indian government.

The traits of pragmatic leaders are already highlighted in this book, and Modi fits the bill here. When he decided to take up the Ram Temple construction, a controversial project all his predecessors have failed at or completely avoided, he was laser-focused on getting it built! As of January 2024, it was reported that 100% of the Ram Temple Project has been completed.

After presenting the concrete evidence in this book that India is surely on the right path to clinch the superpower status, if anyone is still doubtful about this possibility, we would like to present five opportunity indices India currently enjoys over other nations:

- **Huge population:** India's population is estimated to be 1.43 billion (2023). This is a huge market size when compared to other nations or continents. For instance, the entire European Union, with 448 million people, is one-third of India's population, and Africa's population, estimated at 1.47 billion is slightly bigger than India's, while the whole of South America has only 441 million people. Interestingly enough, India also has more people than China, making India the most populous country in the world. The median age in the country is 28.4 years old (2023) and the average life expectancy for men and women is 70.5 years old and 73.6 years respectively. This translates into the fact that an average Indian has nearly 50 years that they could contribute to the labor pool and the country won't experience a shortage of labor should its productivity double or even triple in the next 10 years. According to recent estimates, about 36.3% of the Indian population lives in urban areas, and a large percentage of them are becoming cash-heavy, well-educated middle-class people. As already discussed in this book, becoming an economic powerhouse will cause more migrations to the urban communities, just as the case was in China which has been recording a steady increase in net migration from the rural areas to the urban areas since 1960. Like in China, Indian labor is cheap and knowledgeable in every aspect of the economy.

- **Growth-inducing foundations:** The existing legislations, reforms, and laws in India, that were laid down by successive governments would serve as the growth-inducing foundations upon which other future, necessary reforms would be built. The newly evolving India is far different from what it used to be in the 1960s or 1970s. The New India has shown incredible resilience and it is positioned to take on more transformations to be able to emerge greater and more influential among the comity of nations. This could only be achieved through the dedicated efforts of a transformational leader.

- **Well-educated labor force:** At the moment, the adult literacy rate is 67.77% in rural India while it is 84.11% in urban India. With a 96% adult literacy rate, China has demonstrated that when a nation becomes affluent, educating its citizens won't be any hassle at all. Despite its late investment in education, it is evident that India is already catching up with China, and it may not be long before raising its literacy rate to 97% could be achieved.

Unlike other Asian nations such as Japan, South Korea, and China where billions of dollars are spent on English education, India's English-speaking labor force is already ahead in this respect. This entails that little or no investment would be required to customize foreign technologies transferred into the country since most of these technologies are coded or built-in English, and there wouldn't be many instances of losing vital aspects of their functionalities or features in translations.

- **Strategic location:** India is centrally located in the middle of Asia and this strategic location comes with some blessings. The country enjoys close contact with the West, Asia, Africa, and Europe which, in turn, provides close trade access. More so, the strategic proximity to those continents offers India an ample chance to sell its goods/services to its consumer markets. This could be done after signing some trade agreements with countries on those continents. Because of its central location, India is never far away from affordable talent sources or pools. When it reaches its peak performance and requires additional labor, India could simply tap from some of the countries around it, bringing qualified professionals to operate its industries from China, South Korea, Japan, Singapore, and Europe. Most importantly, the Indian Ocean, which gets its name from India, continues to be a trading hub, and it is currently being accessed by other nations such as the United States, Japan, Australia, China, the United Kingdom, etc. for trade and maritime security purposes. Through the Indian Ocean, the country is connected to Africa via Tanzania; this is a great location because India should become an export-oriented nation as it already has the trade routes necessary for distributing its goods/services.

- **Mutually beneficial foreign relations:** Since its independence until the early 1980s, India's foreign policy has been likened to a sitting-on-the-fence approach. However, having fought wars with China and Pakistan, and seeing the possible opportunities in striking up alliances with other nations, both economic and military partnerships, India has been gradually expanding the scope of its foreign relations, and that has in recent years caused it to mingle with nations such as the United States, Australia, China, and so on. So far, India doesn't have many diplomatic enemies, and that could play to its advantage when it starts to seek foreign markets for its finished goods/services overseas.

What we think the Indian electorates would do is weigh the pros and cons of their actions when the 2024 general election comes up. Would they be willing to give Modi the continuity he seriously needs to complete his transformative works in India? Or would they be trying to throw away the bath water but with the baby in it? Naturally, when there's a change of dispensation, there will also be a corresponding change in policies and style of governance. No one can tell if a new set of leadership other than Modi would be inaugurated in 2024, but the stake is quite high to let India derail from its current rate of economic development.

Due to his sterling performance as two-termed prime minister, Modi has consequently raised the bar about what transformative qualities the next prime minister of India should display or embody. Indian people may be unwilling to elect any political officials who could end up slowing down the country's current socioeconomic progress, those who may unwittingly take the country back to the Dark Ages.

What happens in 2024 is in the hands of the Indian electorates – they could either decide to keep Modi in power and watch him advance India towards superpower status or take a risk bringing in another, untested leader that may wind back all the economic progress made so far. As it turns out, the 2024 general election will be the litmus test for India's economy's chance of survival, expansion, and further transformation.

Chapter 13

Postscript: What We Hope Will Happen (and Not Happen) Next

Neither of us lives in India but it is very much in our minds and hearts. As the saying goes: you can take an Indian out of the country but you cannot take the Indian out of him – which is very much true of us. We have written this book with the belief that India is very much on the cusp of fulfilling its tryst with destiny beyond even Nehru's hopes, of becoming a superpower along with China, the United States, and the European Union. However, it is not a certainty and one of the critical variables is that of leadership.

We hope that the Indian electorate will choose wisely as they have done time and time again. We have put together the case for a transformational leader and analyzed who among the current leaders can rise to the challenge. Our analysis suggests that there is no alternative other than Narendra Modi at the moment. And based on historical examples, he gets another 10 years to complete what he has begun: India's transformation – economic, social, technological, and institutional. We certainly hope that others will eventually come forth or learn from his example to become worthy successors.

What we hope will not happen is that successive governments, whether under Modi or otherwise, lose the will or are unable to carry out the tough reforms or complete India's transformation over the next 20 years. India today is very much aspirational, as well as impatient. Expectations also rise with improvements in economic and social conditions. Therefore, the need of the hour is to rise to the challenge and press on until the destination is reached, whichever government comes in place next.

It is a fact that all the achievements of Narendra Modi mentioned in this book are pretty much works in progress. His profound contributions to India's growth have been uniformly recognized by international institutions such as the World Bank, the UN, and the IMF. For people to fully reap the benefits of Modi's socioeconomic policies, he needs, at least, an additional five years to complete his enormous reforms and projects.

Some of Modi's unfinished businesses or projects, as we have discovered, include:

- **Energy transition:** India can no longer burn coal and oil to obtain the energy required to power its industrial revolution. And having pledged significant support for COP 21, the Modi government still has a lot of work to do in the transition of India's energy from coal/gas to renewable or clean energy sources. It is estimated that coal still accounts for 60% of energy generation in India. Hence, India's National Electricity Plan targets building some new thermal power plants by 2027, except those that are already under construction. There is a proposal under consideration that will guide India into achieving

53% power generation of its power/energy from non-fossil sources by 2027, all developed locally.

- **Socioeconomic Reforms:** There are still some reforms that should be designed and implemented by India to guarantee that its current development or growth rate is sustainable and subsequently improved upon. A number of the FDIs require further liberalization; investors should enjoy ease of doing business in India and the remainder of those difficult bottlenecks should be eliminated.

- **Health Coverage Expansion:** As India's population grows, the health requirements of its people will simultaneously increase. Though some progress has been recorded in this sector, a lot of work is still needed in all areas of healthcare delivery so that everyone in the country can have equal access to high-quality healthcare. More hospitals and clinics are still needed to increase the number of beds per 1000 patients. Currently, India approximately has 1.4 beds per 1000 patients. Compared with China (an equally populous nation), there are 6.7 beds per 1000 Chinese patients.

- **Other Reforms and Projects:** More reforms are still required in education, judiciary, manufacturing, banking and finance, etc. Some of the projects the Modi government is working on are scheduled to be completed after his second tenure ends. To ensure that such landmark and useful projects are not abandoned by the next government, if it is not Modi's, the 2024 general election offers a unique opportunity for the Indian people to salvage their country through their voting power.

The Indian electorates have always chosen their leaders based on their convictions that such leaders could selflessly serve them. Modi has demonstrated that he has what it takes to lead India to its future glory when it eventually becomes a superpower. The journey ahead is long and tedious and India requires a hardworking and dependable leader to get the job done.

Bibliography

Ajit Deshmukh. "Digital Transformation in the Indian Financial Sector." The Times of India. The Economic Times - The Times of India, https://timesofindia.indiatimes.com/

Al Jazeera. '"INDIA": What You Need to Know about India's Opposition Alliance', n.d. https://www.aljazeera.com/

Archie Brown. 'Gorbachev and Economic Reform'. In The Gorbachev Factor, by Archie Brown, 130–54, 1st ed. Oxford University PressOxford, 1997. https://academic.oup.com/

Ashish RAJADHYAKSHA, et al. Country Profile: India. International Federation of Arts Council and Culture Agencies (IFACCA), Aug. 2013, https://asef.org/wp-content/uploads/2020/10/WorldCP-India-Country-Profile.pdf.

Business Today. 'PM Modi Most Popular Leader Globally; Overtakes Biden, Trudeau: Survey', 21 January 2022. https://www.businesstoday.in/

Cerra , Valerie, and Sweta Chaman Saxena. "What Caused the 1991 Currency Crisis in India?" IMF Staff Papers, vol. 49, No. 3, 2022, https://www.imf.org/en/Home

Corporate Finance Institute. 'Four Asian Tigers', 22 November 2023. https://corporatefinanceinstitute.com/resources/economics/four-asian-tigers/.

Dipanjan Roy Chaudhury. "India's Foreign Policy: With Landmark Deals, Manmohan Singh Government Promised Much, Delivered Little." The Economic Times, 23 Feb. 2014. The Economic Times - The Times of India, https://economictimes.indiatimes.com/

Ellen Ellis-Petersen, Hannah, and Hannah Ellis-Petersen South Asia correspondent. "India Overtakes China to Become World's Most Populous Country." The Guardian, 24 Apr. 2023. The Guardian, https://www.theguardian.com/international

Encyclopædia Britannica. 'Mao Zedong.', 22 December 2023. https://www.britannica.com/

Federico Neiburg. National Character. 2015. https://www.researchgate.net/publication/323839448_National_Character

Global Gender Gap Report 2023. World Economic Forum, June 2023, https://www.weforum.org/

Green Business Certification Inc. 'India after COP21: Goals and Accomplishments', 27 June 2017. https://www.gbci.org/

Hindustan Times. 'India Losing $1 Trillion Annually to Corruption: Study', 3 September 2014. https://www.hindustantimes.com/

HISTORY. 'Soviet Union - Countries, Cold War & Collapse', 20 March 2023. https://www.history.com/

Hoover Institution. 'The Marshall Plan', n.d. https://www.hoover.org/

India Today. 'Opposition Names Alliance "I.N.D.I.A": Here Is What It Means', n.d. https://www.indiatoday.in/

Jahangir, Aziz, and Cui Li. 'Explaining China's Low Consumption: The Neglected Role of Household Income'. International Monetary Fund, Working Paper No. 2007/181, 1 July 2007. https://www.imf.org/external/pubs/ft/wp/2007/wp07181.pdf

Jong-A-Pin, Richard, and Jakob De Haan. "Political Regime Change, Economic Liberalization and Growth Accelerations." Public Choice 146, no. 1/2 (2011): 93–115. https://www.jstor.org/

Lauren Frayer and Mary Childs. "India, Farming, and the Free Market." NPR, 16 Apr. 2021. NPR, https://www.npr.org/

Make In India | Prime Minister of India. https://www.pmindia.gov.in/en/

Manoj Kumar. 'Exclusive: India Needs Land, Labor Reform to Aid Manufacturing - Chief Economic Adviser'. Reuters, 4 March 2019, sec. Business. https://www.reuters.com/

Ministry of Information and Broadcasting Government of India. Employment Situation in New India: Indicators back to pre-Covid levels but government keen on improving situation further. PDF File. February 24, 2022. https://static.pib.gov.in/WriteReadData/specificdocs/documents/2022/feb/doc202222418201.pdf

Neiburg, Federico. National Character. 2015. https://www.researchgate.net/publication/323839448_National_Character

Ninan, T.N. The Turn of the Tortoise: The Challenge and Promise of India's Future. Penguin-Random House India, 2016.

'PM Modi Most Popular Leader Globally; Overtakes Biden, Trudeau: Survey', 21 January 2022. https://www.businesstoday.in/

RAJADHYAKSHA, Ashish, et al. Country Profile: India. International Federation of Arts Council and Culture Agencies (IFACCA), Aug. 2013, https://asef.org/wp-content/uploads/2020/10/WorldCP-India-Country-Profile.pdf.

Sumathi C P, and Savitha H S. "IMPACT OF DIGITALIZATION ON INDIAN ECONOMY." Seshadripuram Journal of Social Sciences (SJSS) , vol. Vol 2, no. Issue 1, Nov. 2019, https://mcom.sfgc.ac.in/

Tagem, M.E. Abrams, and Kunal Sen. 'Unlocking The Mystery of Domestic Savings.' UNU WIDER (blog), 2 October 2020. https://www.wider.unu.edu/

The Economic Times. 'Explained: The Rise and Fall of the UPA', 1 December 2021. https://indianexpress.com/

The Economic Times. "How the Middle Class Will Play the Hero in India's Rise as World Power." 9 July 2023. The Economic Times - The Times of India, https://economictimes.indiatimes.com/

The Indian Express. 'Modi Frames 2024 Battle: Fight against Corruption, Nepotism, Appeasement; Singles out a "Parivaarvadi" Party', 15 August 2023. https://indianexpress.com/

The Indian Express. 'Explained: The Rise and Fall of the UPA', 1 December 2021. https://indianexpress.com/

The Indian Express. 'Modi Frames 2024 Battle: Fight against Corruption, Nepotism, Appeasement; Singles out a "Parivaarvadi" Party', 15 August 2023. https://indianexpress.com/

Made in the USA
Columbia, SC
02 December 2024

47211444R00104